"Kathy Coffey has given us a book of American saints for the era of Pope Francis. Where her title metaphor focuses on the American penchant for exploring frontiers, the book's saints—some canonized, others simply recognized—made me also think of Francis' metaphor of going out to the streets of our world. The saints Coffey covers, in brief readable chapters, are all 'gutsy realists'—a memorable phrase used to describe Sr. Dorothy Stang. And all wonderfully human, warts and all. I learned about saints I'd never known, and learned more about others I thought I knew. In the end the book made me think of all the saints among us in this country—so much good news to counter all the bad news that fills our headlines and our heads."

> —John F. Kane
> Emeritus Professor of Religious Studies
> Regis University

"Uh-oh. Here comes marching in a book that won't ever again let us say, 'But the saints aren't anything like us.' Read, if you dare, about the courageous, cantankerous, saintly people who lived in America in their time, but changed the world for all time."

> —Kathy M̄ ⸳ of
> ʾumn *The Story and You*

"Kudos to Kathy Coffey for this collection of 'open, sociable, normal, happy companions,' just the kind of saints Pope Francis says we need. In her characteristically engaging and entertaining prose, Coffey helps us entertain the notion that the path toward sainthood is the very ground on which we stand. Be prepared for the spaciousness that emerges in these stories, both in the vast terrain of landscape these men and women traversed and in their very souls. It is in these wide open places that God enters, grace abounds, and lives are transformed in love."

—Mary Stommes, editor of *Give Us This Day*

When the Saints Came Marching In

Exploring the Frontiers of Grace in America

Kathy Coffey

LITURGICAL PRESS
Collegeville, Minnesota

www.litpress.org

1   2   3   4   5   6   7   8   9

Library of Congress Cataloging-in-Publication Data

Coffey, Kathy.
    When the saints came marching in : exploring the frontiers of grace in America / by Kathy Coffey.
    pages cm
    ISBN 978-0-8146-3718-0 — ISBN 978-0-8146-3743-2 (ebook)
    1. Christian saints—United States—Biography.   2. Christian biography—United States.   3. United States—Church history.
I. Title.

BX4659.U6C64   2015
282.092'273—dc23
[B]

                                                        2014027642

For my grandson, Henry Joseph
May you walk always among heroes such as these

Contents

Introduction

True holiness is completely unself-conscious. You wouldn't have the slightest awareness of its existence in you. Besides you will not care, for even the ambition to be holy will have dropped as you live from moment to moment a life made full and happy and transparent through awareness.

— Anthony de Mello

The starting point is always the goodness of God. God's creative genius peopled the fresh terrain of the United States with remarkable women and men. They lived in our country; they walked its paths. They climbed our hills and mountains, sailed our seas, heard our birdsong, looked for stars in our vast skies. They smelled the rain falling on our prairies and forests. Junípero Serra, a Franciscan, and Kateri Tekakwitha, a Native American, would've found all outdoors a temple. Eating our food, speaking or learning our language, they worked hard, laughed long, and prayed often.

We in the United States are fortunate to brush elbows with many saints who grew and flourished here. As we explore their stories, it's intriguing to imagine them sitting down together at a heavenly banquet, unbounded by the usual human constraints. Their shared values, hopes, beliefs, and actions are strong membranes connecting them beyond time and space. Joining them are their companions, families, and all the marvelous people who unfortunately couldn't fit into this book.

Elizabeth Ann Seton and Pierre Toussaint exchange news about their parish, St. Peter's in New York City; she thanks him for donations to the orphanage staffed by her sisters. Katharine Drexel and John Neumann chat about their hometown, Philadelphia. Marianne Cope, the first to admit alcoholics to the hospital at a time when they were jailed instead, thanks Bill W., Dr. Bob, and Sr. Mary Ignatia for founding Alcoholics Anonymous. Martin Luther King Jr. and Cesar Chavez discuss with Henry David Thoreau his essay, "On Civil Disobedience." He preferred jail to paying a tax that would finance the Mexican War and extend slavery; his stance on resisting injustice underlay their movements. Rose Hawthorne Lathrop and Elizabeth Ann Seton compare notes on their shared experiences of being widowed, converting to Catholicism when it was most unpopular, losing a child, and constantly caring for the sick. Frances Cabrini and John Neumann discuss immigration with contemporary experts and marvel that the issues of their day still have not been resolved. Thea Bowman and Katharine Drexel roll their eyes about black women being denied admission to religious communities in the early

1900s. Sister Mary Luke Tobin and Rachel Carson measure women's progress in the arenas they pioneered: church and science. Dorothy Day and Helen and Cesar Chavez reminisce about their visits to each other, and Day's imprisonment in 1973 for picketing several California vineyards. Dorothy Stang and the sisters martyred in Liberia talk with Jean Donovan, Ita Ford, Maura Clarke, and Dorothy Kazel about the ties that bound them so closely to their people, they couldn't leave their missions even when their lives were endangered.

Those who've had only a nodding acquaintance with hunger and thirst cannot fully appreciate the feast described in Isaiah 25:4-6, covered with rich foods and fine wines. To add a conversation with this cast of characters would make it a five-star banquet indeed!

No book on the North American saints would be complete without mentioning the splendid depiction on the tapestries at the Los Angeles Cathedral. There, Serra and Seton rub elbows with Peter, Mary Magdalene, and Thomas More. They take their place in that great company that focuses all its attention and energies on the altar, the Christ before them. From both sides of the cathedral they press forward, intent on one goal.

Their visible engagement would be tarnished by comparing it to any other crowd, pushing into a sale, a sports event, or a concert. Their hands are often folded in concentration; their eyes light with anticipation of an unfolding feast. None of the saints are actively doing anything else, for now they have set aside their exhausting work with the poor, their academic achievements, their reforms and foundations. Only one goal matters: what Thomas Merton calls "a communion with God's own light and truth."[1]

The documentary *Divining the Human* shows the process of creating the tapestries. In a juxtaposition of earthly and heavenly, the music of "Pange Lingua" and "Veni Creator Spiritus" drifts over hard hats and scaffolds, clanking metal and the freeway's roar. Lead artist John Nava, a committee of liturgists, those who lay cement or tile, drill, sew hems, install lighting: these too are all part of the communion of saints. Mingled in with the saints depicted on the walls are ordinary citizens of Los Angeles: a little boy in tennis shoes, a girl in jeans, a businessman in a suit. Indeed, ordinary Californians were the models for the saints, and they reflect on what that meant: "Their qualities aren't unattainable or magical." "Becoming a saint is a long process, not just 'Bingo!'" "The Communion of Saints says, 'I belong.'" The saints on the tapestries mirror the assembly, which may explain why some of the first viewers got goose bumps. They were seeing themselves. Underlying the art are the biblical phrases, "See, God's dwelling is among mortals. God will dwell with them. They will be God's people and God will be with them." Small and insignificant as humans sometimes seem, they are nonetheless precious, transcendent saints-in-the-making.

Lest anyone consider them superheroes, let's remember that saintly people walk with all the longing and limitation, reluctance and resistance of ordinary human beings. They share (and have documented in their letters and journals) the failures, fears and frustrations, effervescent joys, and stinging pains of all humanity. Looking *way* back in church history, the fifth-century Council of Carthage insisted that saints remain sinners who rely on God's mercy. If not, they'd be too distant to imitate. And isn't that the point?

A question that arises naturally in this context is, what makes North Americans unique in the larger communion of saints? It must be said first that European encroachment came at the terrible price of decimating native Americans who had first explored these lakes and canyons, mountains, and shores. Typical of our nation's settlement and growth was a fluidity, vitality, and sense of possibility previously unknown in Europe. Historian Daniel Boorstin comments, "By the early 19th century, in crowded, pre-empted Europe, 'No Trespassing' signs were everywhere; control by government covered the map. America offered a sharp contrast."[2]

From the beginning, communities existed before government. Passengers on the Mayflower ship or wagon trains headed West had to create their own systems of order to protect and help each other. Private initiative cleared the fields, raised the barns, and dragged the wagons uphill. The needs of the new country presented a "vast opportunity free of ancient walls between classes, neighborhoods and nationalities."[3]

Advancement wasn't determined by guild, the unearned privilege of aristocracy, or the ruling monopoly, but by hard work, perseverance, skill, and dumb luck. From its beginnings, the country was a hospitable environment for holiness. New England especially showed "reforming effervescence" for multiple causes: tax and prison reform, abolition, education, women's rights.[4] "Seldom has such a large proportion of citizens been so alert to measure the community against its best possibilities." So when Elizabeth Seton's Sisters of Charity took over orphanages sunk in debt, filled with neglected and mistreated children, they not only stood squarely within the American tradition. They naturally invited others to join them in the enterprise.

The frontier has always been vital to the North American experience. Before the first European settlers hovered the potential of the unknown, the gleam of possibilities to explore. *The Great Gatsby* concludes with these lines as the narrator looks at the eastern shore: "Gradually I became aware of the old island here that flowered once for Dutch sailors' eyes—a fresh, green breast of the new world. Its vanished trees . . . had once pandered in whispers to the last and greatest of all human dreams; for a transitory enchanted moment man must have held his breath . . . face to face for the last time in history with something commensurate to his capacity for wonder."[5]

Old World nations knew clearly defined boundaries. But the sense of geography in the new country was vague at best. "The map of America was full of blank places that had to be filled."[6] This unique mix of hope and illusion became fertile ground. On the frontier comes the freedom to break with the past, pushing beyond the boundaries.

Few clucking rulers murmured, "It can't be done." Call it, if you will, less of a "wet blanket effect." Americans often seem happiest when on the move, and this was certainly true of John Neumann or Frances Cabrini—who began as immigrants, and served their new country by difficult journeys through it.

For all these reasons, this book broadens the idea of frontier to unexplored realms of holiness. As Joan Chittister and Rowan Williams write in *Uncommon Gratitude*, "The saint is someone who starts a chain reaction of new perception in the world, who reinforces, even among those who don't or can't yet believe, the confidence that there's more to us all than we have suspected. . . . They keep the doors of vision open when everything and everyone seems to want to close them."[7] They fit General Dwight Eisenhower's description of the ideal soldier, who "must have a darn strong tinge of imagination—I am continuously astounded by the utter lack of imaginative thinking . . ."[8]

The focus here is on the "explorers" in many realms: civil rights, science, education, health care. In the North American context, the quote from Revelation 21:5, "Behold, I make all things new," takes on richer meaning. The people profiled here went into what some would term North America's "hellholes": the raw frontier, the leper colony, the squalid slum. There they brought the vigorous, transforming energy of the resurrection.

God promises the people, "Sing and rejoice, daughter Zion! Now, I am coming to dwell in your midst" (Zech

2:14). While God dwelled among humans most brilliantly as Christ, God comes again and again in different ways, responding to the people's needs at specific times. Through the faces, intelligence, souls, hands, hearts, and feet of those profiled in this book, God is so passionately enamored of human beings, that God chooses to dwell with them over and over.

Seeing things askew with humanity, God doesn't send some spectacular intervention of special effects. Instead, "The great events of this world are not battles and elections and earthquakes and thunderbolts . . . [but] babies, for each child comes with the message that God is not yet discouraged with humanity but is still expecting good-will to become incarnate in each human life."[9]

And so a baby was born to the Bowman family in Mississippi, to the Judge family in New York, the Chavez family in Arizona. With a tiny infant began a new act, a stunningly new development, a frontier that had never before been explored. Not only did these pioneers make unique contributions to the American scene; they also kept reinventing themselves. Eventually, they crafted their lives into such works of art that people around them noticed, and commented.

Consequently, any book such as this compiles the work of previous scholars who have worked far longer and in much greater depth on their subjects. But as artist Michael O'Neill McGrath wrote, quoting St. Francis de Sales, patron saint of writers, we all simply rearrange the flowers given us by those who came before, into new and different bouquets.[10]

Questions for Reflection or Discussion

As you begin, explore your own notions of holiness by describing someone you consider whole, human, fully alive, sensitive to God's action in his or her life—but *not* perfect.

1

Junípero Serra

As happens so often when we stop to regard God's work,
there is nothing to do but wonder and thank God.

— Mollie Rogers, *Foundress of Maryknoll Sisters*

A common blessing given by parents to their children
in Mallorca at the time Miguel Serra grew up there
was "May God make a saint of you."[1] In Fr. Serra's case, it
happened—by a long, uncharted path. The story of a boy
from a small island in the Mediterranean, who founded
the long chain of California missions, may have begun
when he admired the beauty of creation: almond trees
flowering, glimpses of blue sea, olive orchards he'd harvest
with his father.

Later he would study the medieval Franciscan phi-
losopher Duns Scotus, who delighted in God creating
the world and becoming human not to somehow offset
sin, but because of God's generous, outreaching nature.
Scotus also believed that God created individuals by name,
delighting in their individuality. That philosophy would

later play out in Serra's respect for the Native Americans he'd meet across the sea.

After joining the Franciscan community, Serra chose the religious name "Junípero," or clown of God, after one of St. Francis's first companions, a man filled with laughter, glee, and pranks. It seems an odd choice for a serious, academic sort, but perhaps he remembered Francis's comment, "Would . . . that I had a forest of such Junipers!"[2]

By 1742, Serra had been ordained, studied hard, and received his doctorate at age twenty-nine. He was a popular professor, retreat director, and preacher who emphasized God's expansive mercy. But he began to see warning signs all over his island: the Spanish army constantly conscripting his students for their war machine, a depressed economy, crop failures due to drought, widespread starvation. Like many people of his time, Junípero had always been eager to become a missionary. When he heard a call to go to the New World, he seized the chance, despite being considered "older," at age thirty-five. In an odd arrangement, the Spanish government paid the priests' expenses, helping to cement their settlements in Mexico and California, warding off encroaching Russian settlement.[3]

Serra didn't have the heart to tell his parents and sister he would probably never see them again, so he said goodbye in a letter sent through a relative. Usually articulate, he admitted, "Friend of my heart, I lack words to tell you how much sorrow I feel in leaving you. . . . I wish I could share with them [his parents] the great joy that fills my heart. Surely then they would encourage me to move forward and never turn back."[4] He traveled with Fr. Palou, his friend, former student, and later biographer.

Serra's ninety-nine-day voyage there would occur two hundred years after the Dominican Bartolomé de Las Casas called attention to Spanish atrocities among the native peoples. The first conquistadors massacred the natives or forced them into brutal enslavement. De Las Casas had the audacity to suggest that genocide might not make the Christian faith attractive to "Indians," and that, indeed, they should be treated well. His influence led to abolishing slavery and eventually to slightly more humane treatment, recognizing the humanity of native tribes. Paltry as it may seem now, it was advanced compared to the colonial British treatment of slaves.

Serra would spend his first nineteen years in the New World around Mexico City and Oaxaca. There he was introduced to the debate that raged throughout the eighteenth century between friars and government authorities about the native populations. Some thought the friars infantilized the natives, whereas the Franciscans simply wanted to protect them.[5] (Understandable when some Spanish soldiers were nicknamed "Exterminators.") The natives caught in the middle of the debate were oddly voiceless.

Serra also began practices there that he'd continue as president of the missions in California: learning languages and utilizing hands-on rituals like washing feet and Christmas pageants, building beautiful churches and pitching in on construction. As Kenan Osborne, OFM, says, a key element of Franciscan life is "getting your hands dirty with good cheer."[6]

He finally left for California in 1767 at fifty-four, an age by which most people of his day had retired. After expelling the Jesuits, the Spanish King Carlos ordered Franciscans to establish missions in Alta California. The king's representative sent them to Monterey first, where they were told to name the first mission for the king. (St. Francis could wait until they found the legendary, foggy harbor.) On his way, Serra, walking always with a painful ulcerated foot, the result of a snakebite in Mexico, had his first encounter with natives who had not been in previous contact with any missions. In northern Baja, his writing is filled with reverent wonder for their unashamed nakedness, grace, vitality, and charm. Unique for his time, Junípero also acknowledged that the country was *theirs*. He offered them figs; they gave him fish.[7]

Because two parties were sent by land and two by sea, both arduous routes, there was great joy when they met in San Diego. The ships' crews were dying from scurvy and lack of fresh water; the first "mission" established there was more an outdoor hospital. Their misery was soon compounded by an attack of the Kumeyaay tribe. The Spanish defense was a display of firearms that the natives had never seen, and that became a fairly easy way of conquering California. Serra intervened so that members of the tribe were *not* punished for their attack.

While Serra's writing delights in the smell of sea, the discovery of fresh water and roses, even jokes about the natives wanting his ragged gray habit (because clothing was highly prized),[8] he must have also seen how unrealistic was his dream of native peoples gladly presenting themselves for baptism. A culture based on personal freedom and individuality was reluctant to embrace the missions' highly organized communal living. Despite his relentless optimism, Junípero may have gradually come to recognize that a man nailed to a cross had little appeal to a buoyant, happy people whose abundant resources met most of their needs. Coastal Californians formed the oldest habitation in North America, dating from 11,200 BC, due to a moderate climate, skilled fishing and hunting, and clever cooking of plants, seeds, and nuts.[9]

After San Diego, Serra plunged ahead by sea to Monterey. He said his first Mass there beneath an oak tree revered by legend as the one where a Carmelite had landed in 1602. That first priest, Antonio de la Ascension, had laid down the rules: the religious, not the military, were in charge. As an issue never fully resolved, it remained a constant battle for Serra. But in the initial celebration, he led the singing of "Salve Regina," and displayed a statue of the Virgin Mary he had brought on mule for one thousand miles, who would dazzle the natives and accompany him as he founded Carmel mission five miles south, further from military intrusion. There, they cut down magnificent Monterey cypresses to build the new church and headquarters in 1770.

At the next, San Antonio mission, Serra hung a bell from a tree, and rang it long and loud. Despite his flair for drama, even he must have grinned ruefully when no one responded to his call, "Come." But before Serra's death in 1784, this mission would have the largest population, the first irrigation system in California, an orchestra introduced by a musical Spanish friar, and grapevines that outlasted any other mission's.

Few now know how precarious the California venture was, with the constant possibility of abandoning the whole attempt. So many Spaniards sickened or died, it was hard to see how the natives would ever want to become like them. Because their food supplies came by unreliable ships, the Spanish were much less healthy than the natives who ate the abundant game and fish of the area. (The missions would eventually introduce oranges, olives, and almonds, now staples of the California diet.)[10]

Interestingly, Serra remarked to his superiors that the natives were better Christians than the Spanish soldiers who constantly raped, murdered, and flogged the indigenous people, creating angry resentment about their presence. These atrocities caused Serra to worry that the natives whom he believed were "gentle sheep" could turn into "tigers and lions."[11] One young friar condemned the Spanish violence and pointed to its logical conclusion: "There is not a single mission where all the gentiles have not been scandalized . . . [and] many times on the point of coming here to kill us all."[12]

One example of the tension: Serra's relationship with the arrogant Captain Fages became so venomous that even while journeying through wilderness, they would not speak to each other, and communicated only by letters. (The same leader made an excellent point: that Serra should stop baptizing people until he had enough to feed them.)[13] The enterprise "teetered constantly on the edge of starvation."[14] Supply ships either sank or were delayed, so food was often lost or spoiled.

Finally, in desperation, Junípero made the painful trip to Mexico City to plead his case before the viceroy of New Spain. Getting a surprisingly warm reception by the unusually enlightened ruler Bucareli, Serra laid out a thirty-two-point plan that has been called "the first significant body of laws to govern early California." Forthrightly, he defended the rights of indigenous women, whom few others recognized as even human. He even asked, unless the behavior of Spanish soldiers improved, "what business have we . . . in such a place?"[15]

It's hard to criticize one who so quickly condemned himself. He recognized the inherent contradictions of his ministry—needing more Spanish soldiers for defense, at the same time knowing they'd prey on native women. In one dark mood, he even pointed out that despite innumerable blunders, right can come from wrong. No one then had any idea how diseases introduced by the Spaniards would decimate the native population. During Serra's era, natives died at a rate 50 percent higher than in their years before contact with Europeans. One scholar points out the great paradox of the missions: they brought both protection and exposure.[16]

Many have pointed out that Serra had the unique blend of qualities that could keep the California missions afloat in distress. If nothing else, he had staying power, remaining when many others despaired, left, or went crazy. Carmel became his base, and he eventually founded nine missions, leaving it to his successors to establish the rest of the twenty-one. He wanted to bring people eternal life, at great personal cost, unaware they might have been quite happy without his version.

Toward the end of his time on earth, Serra became more reflective, perhaps questioning whether he had fulfilled his life's purpose, wondering how history might judge him. The jury may still be out on that one—and how could he ever have predicted the startling growth of Los Angeles, San Diego, or San Francisco? It's probably inevitable that *someone* would've discovered and exploited the indigenous cultures of California, and, hard as it is to believe, the Spanish were better than some colonizers. After their two hundred years of conquest, half the native population remained, whereas in areas conquered by British and Americans, it dwindled to 6 percent.

Like most human beings, Junípero was complex. As he himself wrote of his experience, "I am quite aware of the enormous difference there is between reading about it and actually going through it."[17] One has to admire the dedication of a 5-foot-tall, 110-pound man with a badly infected foot and lower leg who *walked* 1,000 miles of his 9,000-mile journey. Indeed, when Californians were asked what statue should represent their state in Congress, they unanimously chose Serra.

To judge his religious belief and practice by contemporary standards is anachronistic. Simply because Serra is a controversial figure doesn't mean he can't be a saintly pioneer. His paternalism toward the Indians may have been pragmatic: outside the missions, they'd be thrown into the ranches as slave laborers. Nothing in his writing reflects anything but goodwill toward native peoples, protectiveness of them, and the wonder that stirred when he first met them in 1769.

Questions for Reflection or Discussion

It's good that this book begins with a saint who was so clearly imperfect, as all that follow will be. It's hard to evaluate Serra from another historical time, but given all you've read in this chapter, is it easier to sympathize with him? Why or why not?

If you could've joined Serra in his reflections toward the end of his life, how might you answer his question on how history would judge him? What would you name as his finest legacy?

Further Readings

Donna Genet, *Father Junípero Serra: Founder of California Missions* (Springfield, NJ: Enslow Publishers, 1996).

Gregory Orfalea, *Journey to the Sun: Junípero Serra's Dream and the Founding of California* (New York: Scribner, 2014).

2

Elizabeth Ann Seton

> We know certainly that our God calls us to a holy life.
> We know that [God] gives us every grace, every abun-
> dant grace; and though we are so weak of ourselves,
> this grace is able to carry us through every obstacle
> and difficulty.
>
> — Elizabeth Ann Seton

The curved colonnade of the Watson house is unique
in the Battery area of New York City. Where skyscrap-
ers probe ramrod straight into the sky, this rounded, red
brick colonial seems a quaint anachronism. Businesspeople
in serious suits stride purposefully past it, while swarms
of tourists move toward the Staten Island ferry. Yet this
small place still holds some pulse of the city's and country's
life. Once the home of Elizabeth Ann Seton in a fashion-
able neighborhood facing the Hudson River, it's now the
Church of Our Lady of the Rosary, with a shrine to Seton
at the back. She is rightly heralded as the first native-born,

North American, canonized saint. Not a martyr, she lived instead with many heartbreaks: the deaths, before she was four, of her mother and infant sister, then, when she was twenty-nine, of her husband, and finally of two daughters as young girls. Late in life, she marveled that she had lived through it all.

Contemporary issues that would've interested her swirl around this small oasis in New York traffic. Immigration would've concerned her because when her husband William Seton sickened, the medical recommendation was that a few months in Italian sunshine would restore his health. Instead, the Seton party was confined to a lazaretto (a place like prison) because the Italians feared yellow fever. (He actually died of tuberculosis.) Once at the height of society, they quickly became the refugees.

International business thrives here. So too the Seton shipping company had commerce around the world. William had worked with the Filicchi family in Italy for two years, learning the shipping business before he met Elizabeth.

Interfaith dialogue and the ecumenical movement prompted by Vatican II might've amazed Elizabeth, since her conversion made her an outcast of upper-crust society. She agonized over the right path to God, believing there was only one. Many of her Episcopal friends and family rejected her, since Catholics were at the bottom of the social heap, but some friends remained faithful despite what they saw as folly.

New trends in education? She would've gobbled them up, wanting nothing but the best for her students, whether they paid a small tuition or came for free. In the early days of her first school, she, herself would study after classes ended at five o'clock, "stuffing her brain" with math and grammar to teach the next day.

Elizabeth had delighted in the beauty of creation, like the linden trees blossoming along the Hudson, the waterfall and ducks on a pond near the children's playground at Battery Park. She would continue to admire the woods, flowers, and butterflies of her adopted home in the mountains of Maryland.

The biographical details are well known:

Born two years before the American Revolution, Betsey Bayley was the doctor's petite and beautiful daughter, raised in privilege, but still lonely. His remarriage after her mother's death and subsequently seven more children meant Elizabeth had to live with various relatives. When she met Will at age sixteen and married him four years later, she wrote, "My own home at twenty—the world—that and heaven too, quite impossible!"[1] The attractive couple were compatible in many ways: especially charming were duets where she played the piano, and he the violin.

But the idyllic times were short-lived. They had five children in seven years, and Will's shipping business began to fail. Elizabeth tried to help with accounts and her father gave money, but bankruptcy or debtor's prison seemed inevitable. Then Will's father died, and his own health failed. The solution, which most of their friends thought madness, was the Italian climate, voyaging with their oldest daughter Anna, and leaving the four younger children with relatives.

They'd been encouraged to come by his business associates Antonio and Filippo Filicchi, but no one anticipated their terrible forty days jailed in quarantine. Later, Elizabeth would write, "To be sent a thousand miles on so hopeless an errand . . . " Will needed warmth and light; they were confined to a damp, cold dungeon. Despite abysmal conditions, Elizabeth could joke that when the "capitano" poked them back with a stick from speaking too close to the iron grill, "It reminded me of going to see the Lions."[2]

They were finally released to their friends on December 19, 1803, but two days after Christmas, Will died. Elizabeth was left penniless, with five children under eight. It wasn't the first time she'd be undeterred by an apparent dead end. Her plan to return to the United States on February 19 was foiled when the ship's sailing was delayed. She and Anna didn't leave until April 8, and the extra time in Italy may have been crucial to her conversion.

Why was Elizabeth drawn to Catholicism? It was definitely a countercultural path. When she was born, Catholic worship was illegal in the colonies. Catholics weren't allowed to vote, and they definitely were the poorest people of society, mostly recent immigrants, living in squalor. Her sister Mary summed up the common view: "let me be anything in the world but a Roman Catholic . . . dirty, filthy, red-faced—the church a horrid place of spits and pushing." Even Julia Scott, who remained Seton's supportive best friend throughout her life, called Catholicism "folly, madness, bigotry and superstition."[3] Seeing the art and beauty of the Catholic Church in Italy must've been a dramatic surprise. Her Italian friends, especially Antonio, were also significant influences, offering her reading material and encouraging her to convert.

She was especially delighted by the importance given to Mary by Catholics: that had not been part of her Episcopal faith. But it touched some deep chord within a girl whose mother died when she was three: "I felt really I had a Mother which . . . my foolish heart so often lamented to have lost in early days." She was also astonished by the Catholic belief in the Real Presence of Christ in the Eucharist, and the frequency with which they received Communion. She wrote to her sister-in-law Rebecca, who had always shared her spirituality (and who died shortly after her return to New York), "how happy would we be if we believed what these dear Souls believe, that they possess God in the Sacrament."[4] Her experience mirrors that of many Catholics who say they remain in the church primarily because of the sacraments, and who, if they leave, say they most miss the Eucharist.

The cost of her conversion from the Episcopal Church (whose representatives attended her canonization in 1975) to Catholicism was high: ostracism from her family and many friends. She had been close to her eloquent pastor at Trinity Episcopal Church, Rev. Henry Hobart, who challenged her new belief in Eucharist. Their final meeting was "a short and painful visit on both sides."[5] It's hard to imagine an era so hostile to today's ecumenism, but consoling that diverse churches of downtown New York now work together in a project fittingly called the Seton Bridge.

After much agonizing and delay, Elizabeth became Catholic on March 25, 1805. She had anticipated the moment so eagerly that she wrote of her long walk to St. Peter's Church: "Every step counted nearer that street, nearer that tabernacle, then nearer that moment he [God] would enter the poor little dwelling so all his own."[6]

Seton could easily be patron saint of single parenthood, financial anxiety, household drudgery, and bottomless grief. In early widowhood, she had to rely on the charity of others, and wrote, "I have so great a desire if only to taste a bit of bread of my own earnings." Yet every plan for her to start a school or take in boarders seemed to fail disappointingly. Nevertheless, joy in her newfound faith seemed to carry her through the worst. As she wrote Antonio Filicchi, "You have led me to a happiness which admits of no description, and daily even hourly increases my soul's peace."[7]

The only hope for the small family's security came from the offer of Louis Dubourg, the president of St. Mary's College in Baltimore. He wanted Elizabeth to start a school for girls. In fact, he had only two prospective students, his nieces. But he was a charming and persuasive Frenchman and she had nothing to lose.

With her sons studying at Georgetown, Elizabeth and the three girls boarded a boat bound for Baltimore, her daughters reluctant to leave New York. Saying good-bye to the city where she had been so happy, never to return, was difficult for her, too. They saw from the ship the windows of the State Street home in the Battery where she had played duets with Will, and her father's home on Staten Island where she and the children had spent many lovely summers. She wrote to a friend of this farewell, "can the heart swell so high and not burst?"[8] But once before, she had sailed into the unknown, leaving Will's grave behind in Italy. Again, she must have wondered what lay ahead.

Her time in Baltimore proved delightful but brief. Whereas 1,500 mostly despised and poor Catholics lived in New York, 16,000 prosperous, educated Catholics lived in Maryland. The first Catholic cathedral in the country was being built, under the leadership of Bishop John Carroll. He was visionary, enlightened, and inclusive, respected by members of many denominations. (He even proposed Mass in English, a change that wouldn't occur for two hundred years with Vatican II.) Settled with her daughters in a lovely home between two orchards near the seminary, Elizabeth wrote, "in every respect my condition is like a new being."[9] She quickly fetched her sons from Georgetown, and the whole family was reunited. The little school began to grow, and several other women joined in a loose community dedicated to prayer and service. But then a donor gave them land in Emmitsburg, a mountainous, rural area fifty-two miles from the city.

It must've been a hard decision to move there, when all Seton wanted was a larger house in Baltimore. She would miss the city's conveniences, library, and active population, but when anyone suggested "the will of God," she acted quickly. The other women with her began to wear the simple black widow's clothing she had worn since Will's death, and this soon became the "habit" of the first North American religious community of women.

Male clergy tried to force on her the French rule of the Daughters of Charity, but Elizabeth was adamant that nothing should interfere with her "darlings," her children, her first priority. Despite the beautiful countryside, the early years in Emmitsburg were difficult, with constant illness and death, squabbles with tyrannical clergy, financial insecurity, tedious conflict over the rule and leadership, a grueling schedule, brutal cold, fleas, food shortages, and uncertainty about the school. Always the leader, Seton coped with it all, admitting, "Tribulation is my element."[10] Then her beautiful sixteen-year-old daughter Anna began to show signs of the "family enemy," tuberculosis. When she died, Elizabeth was heartbroken; fortunately a compatible priest, her sister Mary, and her friends helped her endure the grief.

When her daughter Rebecca grew critically ill at age fourteen, Elizabeth asked her old friend Julia for a doll, apologizing that it was so expensive, but admitting, "I am extremely fond of them myself." In 1816 Rebecca died within her mother's arms and was buried beside her sister. From her window, Elizabeth could look out at the graveyard—"it keeps up my heart to look over twenty times a day . . . and think no more pain now."[11]

Meanwhile, the sisters were asked to staff orphanages in Philadelphia and New York, a ministry that would eventually expand to hospitals, schools, and social services all over the country. As one sister predicted, their quiet work in a valley would "give such a roar one day that the noise will sound over all America."[12]

Elizabeth tried to get her sons work with the Filicchis, whose devoted friendship tolerated even the boys' incompetence and laziness. Her only living daughter Kit visited Julia Scott in Philadelphia, where her mother's old friend saw many resemblances to Elizabeth—who had, however, laughed more. Friends and relatives who had so cruelly rejected her mother welcomed her, and she marveled at the dancing, ball gowns, and beauties she had left behind at the age of eight. As Elizabeth aged, Kit's letters brought great delight and must've kindled memories of her younger self. Eventually, Kit became a Sister of Mercy, doing prison ministry. Elizabeth died in 1821 at age forty-six. She was canonized in 1975, her vivacious spirit perfectly reflecting the North American frontier of new efforts and reinvented ways.

She could address many contemporary quandaries. Difficult teenagers? Her sons were "a thorn in the heart," of whom she said, "what's a parent to do but pray and dote?" Tedious housework? She shoveled snow off the children's beds in Emmitsburg. Advocacy for the marginalized? She welcomed the first African-American students, and insisted on the education of *girls*, apparently deflecting questions about why they weren't learning simply to embroider.

Toward the end of her life, Elizabeth wrote her old friend Antonio Filicchi, "Could you but know what has happened in consequence of the little dirty grain of mustard seed you planted by God's hand in America!" Orphans fed and sheltered, many children educated, and "nearly 200 souls in our house look for their daily solace of a mother's smile."[13]

Her self-deprecating one-liners could out-quip Stephen Colbert. She called herself the "Old Lady" who simply doled out affection. After founding what would become the American Catholic schools, she dismissed an arduous body of work: "A ruined carcass, bundled up in old shawls and flannels, I never do the least work of any kind."[14]

Elizabeth's humor transcends eighteenth-century piety; her mysticism resonates with the best of contemporary spirituality. When she had lost almost everything—husband, beloved sister-in-law, home, comforts, she wrote drily, "is Poverty and Sorrow the only exchange? . . . Well, with God's blessing, you too will be changed into dearest friends."[15] That is the voice of the spacious soul, welcoming whatever comes, finding even in the worst surprises the mysterious presence of the Holy.

Questions for Reflection or Discussion
How would you describe Seton's appeal to single parents?

How do Seton's life and writings challenge the idea of a saintly person as one who's detached, unemotional, floating piously three feet above the ground?

Further Readings

Joan Barthel, *American Saint: The Life of Elizabeth Seton* (New York: St. Martin's, 2014).

Anne Flood, SC, *Grace & Courage: The Poetic Inner Stream of Elizabeth Seton's Writings* (Vail, CO: Diamond Tail Press, 2011).

Ellin Kelly, ed., *Numerous Choirs*, vol. 1, *The Seton Years* (Evansville, IN: Mater Dei Provincialate, 1981).

3

Pierre Toussaint

The things which make men alike are finer and better than the things which keep them apart.

—Jane Addams

Because the official canonization process is intricate and expensive, a large percentage of the canonized saints founded religious orders. Their members can represent the case in Rome, but it has led to an imbalance: the number of priests and nuns is far disproportionate to the laity in the ranks of the canonized. That's why it's so refreshing to read the story of a married man who worked hard all his life; loved his wife, adopted niece, and many friends; was unfailingly generous to the poor—and did it all in the teeth of racial bigotry. He perfectly fits Pope Francis's desire for more "saints without cassocks and without veils."[1]

While the "journey" theme permeates the lives of many saints, it seems particularly appropriate for Pierre Toussaint. Born a slave in Haiti, he was highly educated and close to the French Berard family who owned him. One of their daughters, Aurore, only five years older, would be his godmother and constant playmate. Many French families owned huge plantations on the island, because they could quickly amass a fortune there, with slave labor and lucrative exports of sugar, coffee, cotton, and cocoa, then return to France and live lavishly. They created "the wealthiest colony the world had ever seen."[2]

Until the whole system began to explode. A half million slaves brought against their will to an island four thousand miles from their home in the Congo and treated despicably by thirty-two thousand whites, government corruption and incompetence, the effects of the French Revolution on its far-flung colonies: these and many other complex influences led to the gradual expulsion of the planters. Various slave revolts began in 1791 and by 1804, Haiti's leader issued an order to slaughter all white people, which was grimly and thoroughly followed. It perhaps explains why it's rare to see white people in the resident population today.

The historical background is complex. Millions of original Arawak people who inhabited Haiti when Columbus arrived would be exterminated by disease and genocide fifty years later. Horrified, the same Bartolomé de Las Casas named in the chapter on Junípero Serra spoke out on behalf of native peoples. Inadvertently, however, he caused a worse crisis. To maintain the New World's vast plantations required slave labor; he suggested the Spanish king authorize importing Africans—which de Las Casas would later regret. To their credit, the church's missionaries pressed for slave protections, but slaveholders largely ignored the resulting legislation, like King Louis XIV's Code Noir.[3]

The daughters of the Berard family were already in Paris for schooling, and the rest of the family, terrified by Haiti's bloodbath, yellow fever, and other atrocities, worsening by 1797, left for New York. Their trading contacts there arranged passage and housing. The family took along five black servants, four of them slaves, including Pierre and his younger sister, Rosalie. It must have been a shock for children (he was fifteen, she was ten) raised in a lush tropical climate to adjust to the city and experience its cold weather. Furthermore, they were wrenched from their families and would never see them again. They had probably never encountered so many white people; in stark contrast to Haiti, New York's black population was only 15 percent. And they must've missed the flowers and vegetation—there were none amidst the city's brick buildings and paved streets.

But one resource Pierre carried in his lineage was his grandmother's genes. Zenobie had been such a capable slave that she ran the Berard plantation, and was given her freedom by a grateful family. Intelligence, self-assurance, dignity, inner strength, and superb competence were all traits she'd pass on to her grandson. She had visited Paris ten times, accompanying the Berard children to school there, and experienced what it meant to be truly free, accepted as an equal. It's quite possible that she arranged for Pierre and his sister to escape to safety.

They also met with danger and racism. But Pierre reinvented himself and saved his white family with remarkable courage and artistry. Apprenticed by his master to learn hairstyling, he turned that skill into hard work and steady income. Indeed, he saved the white Berard family when his master died and the widow was left penniless. Toussaint himself paid off her mounting debts and supported the small family; "his work habits were set early, out of sheer, icy necessity."[4] After 6:00 a.m. daily Mass at St. Peter's Church, where Elizabeth Ann Seton entered the Catholic community, he would accept every invitation to style hair. Often he worked seventy- to eighty-hour weeks, cheerfully and resourcefully. He even managed to pay off the debt for his apprenticeship, in installments, by saving gifts and working relentlessly.

Mme. Berard remarried, but her husband was unable to support the household as effectively as Pierre did. Despairing of all she had lost and seeing it would never be recovered, she developed poor health, and freed Pierre on her deathbed. Unfortunately, she did not free his sister Rosalie. It took Pierre four more years of hard work to buy her freedom, and that of his future wife, Juliette.

They were married in 1811, sharing many interests, friends, and a sense of fun. His gifts of mimicry, song, and dance must have buoyed their household. When his sister Rosalie died of tuberculosis at age thirty, they adopted her infant daughter, Euphemie. For a childless couple, the little girl became a great joy. They provided her with love and security, until she died at age fourteen. The marriage was unusual since Juliette was a full partner, with an equal voice of her own. Their home became a center for music, laughter, and superb food like gumbo. Many white children learned to dance from Pierre's lessons and violin playing.

Meanwhile, the couple were supporting many causes: like Seton's community, who founded a New York orphanage in 1817, destitute friends and acquaintances in the Caribbean, and abandoned boys whom they raised in their home. Not fearing contagion, Pierre crossed the barricades to nurse victims of yellow fever. As an active member of St. Peter's social welfare committee, his exquisite charity and tender compassion were widely known. The oppressive racism in New York prompted the Toussaints to frequently consider moving to Paris, and much correspondence with friends there discusses the options. On the plus side, they would be full, equal members of society. On the negative, he might not earn nearly as much money as he did with his regular clientele in New York.

One of his best American friends was Mary Anna Schuyler, who made notes for his biography, later written by her sister Hannah Lee, a best-selling author. The Schuylers' son William was the son Pierre never had; his death at a young age, shortly after Euphemie's, devastated him. Pierre was so close to their grandson Philip that he took him to his first day of school. His biographer comments on "the little boy with his white hand in the black hand."[47] Pierre seemed to instill confidence in everyone, and was consistently imaginative and fun to be around. Philip Schuyler, husband of Pierre's friend and confidant Mary Anna, said of him, "I have met men who were Christians and men who were gentlemen, but I have only met one who was both. And he was black."[6]

One bizarre story should be included just for the record. When in August 1842, Pierre, Juliette, and a friend tried to attend a liturgy or concert (it's not clear which) at St. Patrick's Cathedral in New York, the usher kicked them out. The president of the board, who knew Toussaint's connections in high society, wrote a letter of apology, though none came from the pastor or bishop. A century after Pierre's death, he was removed from his grave at Old St. Peter's where he was buried with Juliette and Euphemie, and placed in a crypt beneath the altar of St. Patrick's! Ironically, Pierre's Protestant friends admired his faith and helped support his endeavors, especially fund-raising.

New York's Great Fire of 1835 destroyed the fortune Pierre had so carefully built through hard work and investment. Yet his first response to it wasn't despair, but outreach to those suffering dislocation and ruin. He refused help from his friends, and told them to give it to the truly needy. Others knew of his catastrophic losses, but seeing his unshakable trust in God, they realized they needn't panic. He simply went back to work, putting one foot in front of the other. Even with painful arthritis, he faithfully made his rounds on foot, to dress hair and extend tender compassion. So Jesus walked to those who needed him, teaching and healing, then eventually walking to wash feet at the Last Supper and die in Jerusalem.

Meanwhile the Toussaint home became the gathering place anchoring friends from Haiti, France, and the United States. Letters asked the generous couple constantly for help of all kinds: finding a job, paying a seminarian's tuition, locating housing or staff, sending provisions, lending money, nursing the sick, tracing lost relatives. Responding to all the requests must have been exhausting, but Pierre seems to have shown consistent ingenuity, persistence, and good cheer.

However, he never recovered from the shock of Juliette's death in 1851, especially since she was much younger than he. He had been the one to comfort other grieving people; this loss made him inconsolable. When Mary Ann Schuyler died the following year, he wept, saying, "It is all so changed . . . so lonely!" He had visited this wealthy lady daily for thirty years, their deep friendship transcending any barriers of race or social class. Despite his own failing health, he continued the slow walk to daily Mass, since he wasn't allowed to take a bus. He died in 1853; among his last words were "God with me," and the response when asked if he needed anything, "nothing on this earth."[7]

Through eulogies and newspaper announcements, people discovered with surprise the breadth of his charitable giving.

Personal tributes such as this from a French lady are equally touching: "he dressed my hair for my First Communion; he dressed it for my wedding, and for christenings, for balls and parties. At burials, in sickness and in trouble, he was always here." Another complimented "his perfect good taste in dress and furniture—he did not like anything gaudy, and understood the relative fitness of things."[8] The New York *Evening Post* added, "the most courteous and graceful, yet wholly unassuming manners . . . the most perfect gentleman." The *Home Journal* called him "the most respected and beloved Negro in New York."[9] Few would've noticed or mentioned his race in a funeral with all the solemn ritual that would be accorded a prince.

In the early church, and still in some countries, saints were named by acclamation: the people were convinced of their goodness. In this case, a chorus of voices, many of them faithful Protestants, affirmed "excellent Toussaint," "the very, very good man," "the good heart."[10]

On his 2013 trip to Brazil, Pope Francis said, "We need saints to live in the world, to sanctify the world and to not be afraid of living in the world by their presence in it. We need saints that are open, sociable, normal, happy companions."[11] He could've had Pierre in mind. Who would've thought that washing, cutting, and curling hair, and holding up the mirror afterwards could become the stuff of sanctity?

Questions for Reflection or Discussion

If hairdressing could become a path to sanctity, what about other jobs that might not have previously been considered "holy"? Name three possibilities.

What other people whom you know could fit Pope Francis's description in the last paragraph?

Further Reading

Arthur Jones, *Pierre Toussaint: A Biography* (New York: Doubleday, 2003).

4

John Neumann

Don't think that a saint must look saintly in the eyes of humans. . . . Their value is in their hearts.

— Gabrielle Bossis

Alone, age twenty-five, his English shaky, five feet two-and-a-half inches tall, having only one dollar and one scruffy suit of clothes, a man disembarks on Staten Island from a ship quarantined for a week in New York harbor. How often have we heard that typical immigrant story? How quickly would we predict that this unlikely candidate would become bishop of Philadelphia and the first male canonized US saint? Yet this shaky beginning marks the story of St. John Neumann, who arrived on eastern shores in 1836.

Born in Bohemia (now the Czech Republic), he was a quiet, studious child, interested in the sciences and math. "My mother," he said, "used to chide me, and call me book mad, a bibliomaniac." During his seminary studies, he began to read the reports of the missionary Leopoldine Foundation, and Fr. Frederic Baraga and the Redemptorists in America. At the time he would have been ordained in Bohemia, but there were too many priests, as in much of Europe. So he set his sights on America, writing in his journal before leaving, "While pondering last evening on my resolution, separation from home appeared to me so bitter that I burst into tears . . . With no other guide than Thyself, O Lord, I stand on the outskirts of an immense region full of dangers and difficulties."[1]

His gifts of organizing, dedication, and learning languages were exactly suited to a fledgling church early in the country's development. Quickly ordained by a New York bishop grateful to have him, Neumann would soon put his motto into action: "As Christ has His work, we too have ours; as He rejoiced to do his work, we must rejoice in ours also." With the enthusiasm of youth, he poured his energies into his work, exemplifying how at its best, celibacy can be life-giving.

At that time, the Diocese of New York was made up of all that state and one-third of New Jersey. Although many of its two hundred thousand Catholics were German immigrants, there were only thirty-six priests for the whole diocese; three of these were German. Neumann was sent to Buffalo, over nine hundred square miles from Lake Ontario down to Pennsylvania. Sounding dangerously young and naive, he responded to the challenge: "I am a strong Bohemian mountain boy. It will not hurt me."[2]

But the long travel (with his feet not quite reaching the horse's stirrups) and miserable accommodations eventually took their toll. After the rigors of the raw frontier, Neumann's health was precarious and he suffered loneliness. On October 13, 1840, the priest joined the Redemptorist foundation in Pittsburgh, followed a few weeks later by his brother Wenzel, who had also emigrated to the United States and became a lay brother in the order.

Even there the going was rocky. "You had better return to your former missions," the novice master glowered. "You will never persevere with us." Denied almost all the usual spiritual direction and formation, he was shuffled about, moving eight times in his first year. After this arduous novitiate, he became at age thirty the first professed Redemptorist in America. The 1842 event was recorded with a German pun: "In truth, a *new man* [*ein neuer Mann*] for our Congregation."[3]

Later appointed superior of the Redemptorists, he faced a catch-22: huge debt, and great need for new foundations. Successful there, he was consecrated bishop of Philadelphia in 1852. Neumann was so convinced it would be disastrous, he wrote, "If Our Lord gave me the choice either to die or to accept this dignity, I should prefer to lay down my life tomorrow, rather than be consecrated bishop."[4] How appropriate that before leaving Bohemia, he had spent his last mark on the books of St. Francis de Sales, who wrote, "poor widows and village folk are full of goodness and piety, while we Bishops, who are placed upon the Church's heights, are cold and hard. Is there no sunshine able to melt the chilliness of my heart?" ("On Ecclesiastical Perfection").

The Diocese of Philadelphia, then one of the largest and most important in the United States, included two-thirds of Pennsylvania, the western part of New Jersey, and all of Delaware. Neumann's appointment was controversial. The diocesan elite were scandalized by his heavy accent, shabby appearance, and subdued personality, rarely outgoing or vivacious. On one visit to a rural parish, he arrived in a manure wagon. Seated on a plank above the fragrant contents, John joked, "Have you ever seen such an entourage for a bishop!"[5]

Like Pope Francis, Neumann's lifestyle was radically different from that of other bishops, for his methods and manners differed from theirs in many ways. Although dispensed from his vow of poverty, he still practiced it. Like the surprising Argentinian pope, he furnished his residence simply, avoiding the usual splendor. Without a secretary, he answered correspondence personally, and welcomed visitors himself. (It's interesting to speculate on how he might respond to the news of contemporary US bishops building themselves lavish palaces.) On a visit to Germany, "he came back to the house he was staying in soaked by rain. When his host suggested he change his shoes, John remarked, 'The only way I could change my shoes is by putting the left one on the right foot and the right one on the left foot. This is the only pair I own.'"[6]

Waves of immigrants flooded Philadelphia during his leadership: German Catholics escaping wars, Irish Catholics fleeing famine, later Italians and other southern and eastern European Catholics. Neumann's gift for Spanish, French, Italian, and Dutch enabled him to hear confessions in at least six languages. "When Irish immigration started, he learned Gaelic so well that one Irish woman remarked, 'Isn't it grand that we have an Irish bishop!'"[7] (Subtly, he pioneered inroads into the church's vast multiculturalism today.) He actively recruited religious communities to provide the immigrants with necessary social services.

Discouraged by constant conflict with the Know-Nothings (a powerful political group opposed to foreigners and Catholics), intense prejudice, even anti-Catholic riots and arson, Neumann asked to be replaced as bishop, but Pope Pius IX insisted he continue.

He did: with a flurry of activity. The first to organize a diocesan Catholic school system, he increased the schools in his diocese from two to one hundred. The Catechism he wrote was in use for thirty-five years, before being replaced by the Baltimore Catechism. He also wrote many articles for Catholic periodicals. In his eighty months as bishop, he built eighty new churches, and the Cathedral Basilica of Saints Peter and Paul. As inadvertent proof that Neumann did the work of several leaders, Philadelphia was divided into five smaller dioceses a few years after his death.

Neumann died at age forty-eight while doing errands —which seems appropriate for a man named "the common person's saint." This squat, square-faced introvert was canonized in 1977, forever showing the relative unimportance of personal appearance and personality traits. He is buried in St. Peter the Apostle Church in Philadelphia.

Questions for Reflection or Discussion

In what ways does Neumann fit your image of a bishop? In what ways does he differ?

Further Readings

Br. John Neumann, "Bishop John Nepomucene Neumann: An American Saint," *Catholicism.org* (July 11, 2005), http://catholicism.org/john-nepomucene-neumann.html.

"St. John Neumann," *Catholic Online*, http://www.catholic.org/saints/saint.php?saint_id=70#wiki.

5

Julia Greeley

Doing little things with a strong desire to please God makes them great.

—St. Francis de Sales

Who would notice an old black woman, pulling a little red wagon or carrying a mattress on her back, walking Denver streets in the late nineteenth century? As it turns out, *lots* of people noticed. In an era before rapid press coverage, e-mail or instant texting, hundreds would file past her coffin for five hours, paying their respects to a saintly lady. She was the first layperson in Denver's history whose body lay in state before the altar of a Catholic church. Headlines trumpeted the "highest honor ever paid."

Born in slavery, Julia Greeley didn't remember much about her childhood. She bore one obvious scar from her early life, though: the loss of one eye, hit by a slave owner's whip; the socket constantly emitted fluid. She would disguise her inability to read and write by asking children to help: "my glasses aren't good enough." Later Mrs. Theodora Arnold would comment on the injury, "it did seem rather repulsive until her kindness made one forget it."[1]

Her kindness took many creative forms. That red wagon, it turns out, was filled with coal and groceries she had begged, then delivered anonymously to poor families at night, so white people wouldn't feel ashamed about donations from a black woman. At one end might be tucked a doll she'd repair so a child without one would have it.

One of her most ingenious "joys" (she'd never term it charity) was appealing to more fortunate young women for their beautiful dresses. She knew other girls with heavy financial burdens who couldn't afford the clothing for school socials. For them, she'd become Cinderella's fairy godmother. The well-dressed quickly entered into the spirit of the gesture, donating clothes that hadn't been worn much, cleaned, pressed, and often decorated with new ribbons or lace. Serving ice cream at the socials, Julia would sneak peeks at those she'd outfitted, and then report to the donors that they were the "prettiest girls on the floor."[2]

Another stroke of Julia's compassion emerged when a recently widowed dairy owner asked her to keep house and care for his three children. As an adult, Mrs. Arnold, who'd been one of those children, recalled their "first Christmas without Mother." Julia took them to the finest department store to see the lights, and choose a favorite toy. The little girl first tried for something inexpensive, but Julia insisted on buying an expensive (one-dollar) gift—at a time when she was earning ten dollars a month.[3]

Hearing of a sick infant, she'd go to the home, tell the mother to get some rest, and sit up all night, rocking and singing to the baby. At times of death, she'd not only cook for the family, but also find them appropriate clothing for the funeral. For a new baby, she'd scout around until she got someone to donate the buggy the family couldn't afford.[4] Big on leaflets she couldn't read, she'd distribute the *Messenger of the Sacred Heart*, and sell two hundred Catholic almanacs to people who must've wondered how she ever persuaded them to buy those.

Julia had come to Denver as a nurse and servant in the household of the former governor, William Gilpin, who had amassed a fortune in real estate. His wife Julia introduced Julia Greeley to the Catholic community. As Julia would later say, "she gave me sumpin more 'n money; she gave me my faith." After her employment with his family, William would make it difficult for her to find work. (She finally got a job cooking and cleaning for the Jesuits at Sacred Heart Church.) After she worked there, she was always invited to meals at the rectory, and couldn't "possibly wear out her welcome."[5]

With a certain finesse, she wore the habit of a Franciscan tertiary as she was buried by Jesuit friends from a Jesuit parish. Like St. Francis, pointed out Eugene Murphy, SJ, "she had taken Christ literally . . . giving away all to the poor and . . . making melody in her heart." Like

Toussaint, she ignored color barriers in an age when they were far more formidable. As a then high school student commented, "Julia may intercede before the throne of God, for those white people whose floors she scrubbed."[6]

In ill-fitting clothes and shoes that flopped up the aisle, Greeley caused some consternation among the wealthy, who protested her having her own pew at Sacred Heart Church. To his credit, the courageous pastor Edward Barry, SJ, quelled the criticism: "As long as I'm pastor here, Julia is going to keep her pew. [She] can sit any place in this church she wants to." Consistently she'd raise the most money for parish bazaars, even getting the firemen to vote for her in a popularity/beauty contest. She raised $350 (a huge sum then) and won.[7]

As Paul Hallett, a *Denver Catholic Register* reporter, wrote of her relative obscurity, "the sanctity of her life can never become uninteresting, irrelevant, or unimportant." He called her a "one-woman St. Vincent de Paul society." An editor of *America Magazine*, John LaFarge, SJ, named her and Toussaint "hidden martyrs of charity" and black "examples of that moral triumph which we call sanctity."[8]

To some extent, the record on Julia Greeley is sketchy. But enough evidence exists to justify her inclusion among pioneers who traveled to sanctity with small steps. Her service might be seen as an echo of Jesus', who in John 13:2-5 takes off his outer robe to wash the disciples' feet. Ronald Rolheiser adds another dimension to the familiar action. John, he suggests, implies more than simply removing clothing that would get in Jesus' way. The outer garment represents all that separates human beings: their race, gender, religion, political bent, moral judgments, pride, and so on.

Underlying all this is the *inner* garment: our certainty of belonging to God, which enables us to do anything for people who may seem vastly different from ourselves. We are imprinted with "the image and likeness of God inside us, and when we are in touch with this, we can find the strength to wash one another's feet across any divide, . . . and begin to feel sympathy for one another beyond our wounds and differences."[9] Contemporaries may have called her "Old One-Eyed Black Julia," but she saw past such descriptions, or any divisions.

Questions for Reflection or Discussion

Does the story of Julia Greeley persuade you that the path to holiness can be made with small steps, almost invisible to the larger world? Why or why not?

If you know anyone like Greeley, doing similar things today, describe him or her.

Further Reading

Blaine Burkey, OFM Cap, *In Secret Service of the Sacred Heart: The Life and Virtues of Julia Greeley* (Denver: Julia Greeley Guild, 2012).

6

Marianne Cope

People on Molokai laugh now—like other people in
the world, laugh at the same things, the same dilemmas
and jokes.

—Sr. Magdalene, *Cope's nurse*

We of miniscule penances and negligible achievements envy Sr. Marianne Cope. We huddle close to
security; she embarked on uncharted waters for a risky and
unpredictable mission. We admire her clear call when ours
seem muddled, her brisk rolling-up of sleeves to scrub a
filthy hospital when we feel paralyzed by too many choices,
"falling in love with her work" when sometimes we can
barely drag ourselves to ours.

But maybe it's not quite so simple. She writes to her
superiors of "200 afflicted with a horrible disease . . . and
[we] are responsible to a government for our transactions."[1]
Anyone who has stood in line at the DMV or endured
an audit by the IRS can relate. Suddenly we're nodding

in shared frustration: the time-wasting bureaucracy, incompetence, frequent delays, and occasional disregard for human suffering.

Born in Germany, Cope moved as an infant with her family to Central New York. Joining the Sisters of St. Francis of Syracuse at the age of twenty-four, she quickly became a leader in the community. After serving as a teacher and principal, she helped found and administer two hospitals. There, she instituted policies that seem common now but were revolutionary then: accepting patients regardless of race or creed, insisting on patients' rights, and treating "outcasts," such as alcoholics rejected by other hospitals.

The medical protocols she developed there were transplanted to Hawaii when she *cheerfully* volunteered to serve those with Hansen's disease. In 1883, the Hawaiian government was searching for someone to run the Kakaako Receiving Station for people suspected of having leprosy. More than fifty religious communities in the United States and Canada refused. Thirty-five Syracuse sisters volunteered immediately; six actually went. In her letter accepting the request, Cope wrote, "I am hungry for the work . . . I am not afraid of any disease, hence it would be my greatest delight even to minister to the abandoned lepers."[2]

"She always did things with a spirit of joy," her biographer Sr. Mary Laurence says.[3] A tribute to her gracious personality, Cope and the Hawaiian queen became fast friends, despite not knowing each other's language. Sister would spend thirty-five years on Molokai, somehow never finding time to visit the United States, and dying there peacefully at age eighty. "One of the first Hawaiian words Mother Marianne and the sisters must have learned was 'aloha.' . . . Their reputation as the Sisters of Charity preceded them. They were God's aloha."[4]

Kalaupapa, Hawaii, is a peninsula cut off from the mainland by high cliffs and from the rest of the world by the ocean. The sick were cruelly ostracized there, dropped off on the beach by boat, quarantined from their families because the disease was incurable and contagious. While St. Damien had first brought hope there in 1873, Sr. Marianne was able to assure him when he lay dying that his work would continue. Indeed, after his diagnosis with leprosy, the church and the government were afraid to welcome him. Only Cope offered hospitality, after hearing that his contagious condition had made him an outcast. He died in 1889, six months after her arrival, probably confident that the work he began would continue in good hands.

Initially, Cope (the appropriateness of her surname seems obvious) and six other sisters ran the Kakaako Receiving Station outside Honolulu; they also opened a hospital and a school for girls on Maui. In 1888, she and two sisters opened Bishop Home for "unprotected women and girls" on Molokai where about one thousand patients were exiled.

Many of us, seeing the utter misery, might have despaired. "To see the infinite pity of this place," wrote Robert Louis Stevenson, who visited in 1889, "a fool were tempted to deny his God." But seeing the work of Sr. Marianne, he wrote this poem in her honor:

> Reverend Sister Marianne
> Matron of the Bishop Home, Kalaupapa
>
> *To see the infinite pity of this place,*
> *The mangled limb, the devastated face,*
> *The innocent sufferers smiling at the rod,*
> *A fool were tempted to deny his God.*
>
> *He sees, and shrinks; but if he look again,*
> *Lo, beauty springing from the breast of pain!—*
> *He marks the sisters on the painful shores,*
> *And even a fool is silent and adores.*[5]

Beyond making the community clean and safe, Cope must've known, like Dorothy Day and Mother Teresa of Calcutta, that "we are saved by beauty." Artistry might seem the last thing anyone would worry about, overwhelmed by lepers' needs. But Sr. Marianne proposed that large wide-necked bottles, decorated with shells, would make beautiful altar vases. And that was the least of her enhancements. Never did she impose her own penances on others; instead, she made a living hell into a place of order and beauty.

Her artistry flourished—trimming hats for the girls, requesting the latest fashion magazines for their dressmaking, creating lovely bows. As Sr. Antonia Brown wrote, "viewed from the back, one would think they were New

Yorkers." Robert Louis Stevenson echoed the admiration: "As for the girls in Bishop Home, of the many beautiful things I have been privileged to see in my life, they, and what has been done for them, are not the least beautiful."[6]

Many Hawaiian children were torn from their parents, suddenly orphaned. A blind father brought his five-year-old daughter to Sr. Marianne, because he could no longer care for her. Trustingly, the little girl placed her hands into sister's outstretched ones; now she had a tender mother.[7]

Cope's journal tends to be brusque and businesslike, but occasionally the gem appears, as on February 20, 1900: "Received box of silk pieces from England for the leper girls for dressing dolls."[8] Sr. Magdalene, her nurse at the end, commented that initially the "graces of life" seemed irrelevant to Molokai. "'We are lepers,' they told Sr. Marianne. 'What does it matter?' Well, she changed all that. Doctors have said that her psychology was 50 years ahead of its time."[9] As her nurse said in 1941, she brought fun to the colony. Before her arrival, it's a safe bet, there was little laughter on Molokai.

Cope planted flowers and trees despite the lack of rainwater, which had to be saved for washing and drinking. She introduced pears, peaches, avocadoes, and apples to enliven her patients' bland diets. Her gardening efforts echo Isaiah 58:11: "Then the LORD will guide you always / and satisfy your thirst in parched places, / will give strength to your bones / And you shall be like a watered garden, / like a flowing spring whose waters never fail."

When the 1905 earthquake and fire struck San Francisco, an outpouring of aid from other states seemed natural. But how impressive when some of it arrived from Marianne's leper colony! Only one woman in the world could encourage people in such dire straits themselves to think of *others* with problems.[10]

Only one effort backfired, recorded here so Cope doesn't seem like a flawless, inhuman paragon: her early attempt to create a joyous Christmas. Since friends had sent Christmas ornaments, she gathered women to decorate a tree. Sparkling with tinsel and lights, it was unveiled to a funereal silence. The lepers had no idea what it was, or why they should be enthusiastic about it.[11]

What made St. Marianne tick? Most powerfully, in her own unique way, she followed One who, shortly after teaching the principles of the Sermon on the Mount, touched gritty reality. Approached by a leper, he stretched out his hand and cleansed him immediately (Mark 8:1-4). He also promised his friends, "whoever believes in me will do the works that I do, and will do greater ones than these" (John 14:12). As Cope wrote in 1905, the time to do good is short: "Let us make best use of the fleeting moments. They will not return."[12]

A cure for Hansen's disease would not be discovered for another twenty-five years after Cope's death, and the law confining patients to Kalaupapa would not be lifted until 1969. But the seeds she planted, in more ways than one, flourish today. Her legacy thrives in the Hawaiian

Islands, where Franciscan sisters run two major acute-care hospitals, two hospices, numerous health facilities, clinics, and schools.[13] At St. Marianne's canonization in 2012, nine patients from Kalaupapa sat in the front rows, and the fragrance of abundant leis filled the Vatican.

Questions for Reflection or Discussion

Imagine yourself as one of the six sisters who originally accompanied Sr. Marianne Cope to Hawaii. What do you record in your journal or tell your family?

Further Readings

M. Davilyn Ah Chick, OSF, and Malia Dominica Wong, OP, *A Walk with Saint Marianne Cope of Moloka'i* (Syracuse, NY: Sisters of St. Francis of the Neumann Communities, 2013).

Lisa Benoit, "Mother Marianne Cope: A Blessed Among Lepers," *St. Anthony Messenger* (July 2005), http://www.americancatholic .org/Messenger/Jul2005/Feature2.asp.

Carol Ann Morrow, "Kateri Tekakwitha and Marianne Cope: Two New American Saints," *Catholic Update* (October 2012).

Sisters of St. Francis of the Neumann Communities, Saint Marianne Cope, http://blessedmariannecope.org/index.html.

Katharine Drexel

The arc of the moral universe is long, but it bends
toward justice.

— Rev. Martin Luther King Jr.

The beauty of the American Southwest has been captured
by many artists like Georgia O'Keeffe, but what would
Katharine Drexel have seen on her first visits there by train?
Surely the fragrance of piñon pine filled the fresh morn-
ings; the pale green lace of new leaves brushed round adobe
buildings; the azure sky burned with that special light that
has drawn so many artists to this part of the country; the
natives danced with the grace that delights visitors now.
The violet lines of mountains blended into the reddish
shades of mesas, canyons, and rock formations that still
capture and reflect the crimson sunsets. The vast spaces
must've seemed infinite compared to her bustling home
city, Philadelphia.

As a child traveling with her parents, Katie's initial
response to the landscape was not recorded. However, she

was sensitive to the squalor in which native peoples lived. She went with her father to the US Northwest Territories in 1884, and after his death in 1885, donated funds to the St. Francis Mission on South Dakota's Rosebud Reservation. The stories of Native Americans must've fired the young Katie's imagination. She first heard from Fr. O'Connor, a family friend, about the Custer massacre, how treaties had been ignored and native peoples forced into despair on reservations.[1] She would be appalled by their treatment, described in Helen Hunt Jackson's books. But no one could've predicted that little girl would start in 1894 the first mission school in Santa Fe, and one day eventually begin fifty missions for Native Americans in sixteen states.

Many other seeds were sown in her childhood. Her own mother died five weeks after her birth, and her father, an affluent banker, remarried Emma Bouvier in 1860. She and her sisters were raised not only in luxury, but also with concern for the poor. Twice a week, the Drexels distributed food, clothing, and rent assistance from their Philadelphia home. When widows or single women hesitated to ask for assistance, the family sought them out, quietly. As Emma taught her daughters, "Kindness may be unkind if it leaves a sting behind."[2]

Balancing responsibility to the less fortunate ran another current: the round of balls and parties a young woman attends, her social debut in 1879. Dresses and invitations, music and language lessons from private tutors, lavish feasts in sumptuous homes, friendships and laughter. Katharine's lively sense of humor was often self-deprecating; that joy would remain a gift throughout her lifetime.

However, watching her stepmother's three-year struggle with terminal cancer taught Katharine the Drexel money could not buy safety from pain or death. When her father died in 1885, the financial genius left a $15.5 million estate, divided among his three daughters. About $1.5 million went to several charities, leaving the girls to share in the income produced by $14 million—about $1,000 a day for each woman. In current dollars, the estate would be worth about $250 million. Francis had engineered his will to deter fortune hunters, so the estate would go directly to his daughters, their children, and if there were none, to his favorite charities. Since Katharine outlived her sisters, who had no offspring, she inherited it all, and was able to channel large amounts into her causes until her death at age ninety-six.

But it wasn't only about money. Katharine began with donations, but soon decided what was needed more were the *human* resources. She and her sisters went to Europe to recover from their father's death. During a papal audience, she pleaded for missionaries to work with the Native Americans. Pope Leo XIII parried with an astute question: "But why not be a missionary yourself, my child?"[3] Katharine left the room in tears; the pope had touched a chord. Most revelations come gradually, and she had apparently already thought about her future direction. Earlier, she'd worried about her fitness. She'd never been without luxuries and cherished time alone: How could she join a religious community?

Her final decision was trumpeted by a banner headline in *The Philadelphia Public Ledger*: "Miss Drexel Enters a Catholic Convent—Gives Up Seven Million." That May 1889 news, which shocked the city's elite, wasn't quite accurate. She didn't give *up* seven million; she would during the next sixty years give *away* about twenty million. It went to support of her work, building schools and churches, paying the salaries of teachers in rural schools for blacks and Native Americans.

It began in 1891, with the profession of Drexel's first vows as a religious, dedicated to work among the native peoples and Afro-Americans in the Western and Southwestern United States. What quickly followed was the establishment of a religious community with thirteen other women, the Sisters of the Blessed Sacrament.

To appreciate the boldness of their action, it helps to understand that particularly in the South, anti-Catholic feeling and Jim Crow laws still flourished. But even in the North, bigotry continued. When the sisters built a new motherhouse in Bensalem, Pennsylvania, a stick of dynamite was discovered near the site.

A tribute to social justice convictions that flowered long before any had such strength is noted by Benedictine Father Paschal Baumann, archivist at Belmont Abbey in North Carolina: "We do Katharine Drexel a disservice if we view her only in terms of her money. She had a real social policy to go with it. She was working for the advancement of integration, and she made that so clearly a mission of the Church, not just a social policy. When Rome is determining who should be recognized as a saint, it looks not only at sanctity but at *heroic* sanctity. It's going that extra mile, and that is certainly evident in her life. It's just magnificent to have her recognized by the Church. It's such a tribute to all progressive thinkers in issues of social justice."[4]

But that kind of perspective is gained at the end of the story, which those who were living through it didn't yet know. In 1913, the Georgia Legislature, hoping to stop the Blessed Sacrament sisters from teaching at a Macon school, tried to pass a law to prevent white teachers from teaching black students.

Furthermore, "in 1915, when Mother Katharine purchased an abandoned university building to open Xavier Preparatory School [for black students] in New Orleans, vandals smashed every window. . . . In the late 1920s, when Mother Katharine found property in New Orleans for expanding Xavier University, she used a third party as a purchasing agent to keep the transaction from falling through. When the handsome campus was dedicated in October 1932, a priest gazed upon the expensive Indiana limestone buildings and remarked in Latin: 'What a waste!'"[5]

Nonetheless, Drexel made what was possibly her most famous foundation—Xavier University sends more African-

American graduates to medical school than any other university in the country. Despite harassment from the Ku Klux Klan, by 1942 the order had established a system of black Catholic schools in thirteen states, plus forty mission centers and twenty-three rural schools. Realizing that rural schools for blacks needed qualified teachers, she trained Xavier students for education degrees, and then convinced their parents to allow them to teach. Sister Marie Celine Enright, an Irish-born sister of the Blessed Sacrament said of Katharine, "The blacks and Native American people were her pride and joy, but they had never had a chance."[6]

Her biography takes a surprising turn in 1935, when Katharine had a heart attack, and two years later retired as superior general. She had traveled constantly by train and stagecoach, gathering knowledge about the Navajos, the Sioux, and the deplorable state of education for native and black children. Until poor health at age seventy-six forced retirement, she made an annual visit to each of her far-flung foundations (145 missions and 12 schools for Native Americans, 50 schools for black students). And she didn't just supervise passively. As one Franciscan priest wrote, "Very often I met the Mother Superior on her knees scrubbing the porch and sweeping the rooms, the dining rooms and wherever the children went."[7]

It must have been a huge transition for one who had been so dramatically active and always on the move, but from her wheelchair she continued praying for justice to those she had served so long. She had wanted a more contemplative life, and she spent her last twenty years in prayer. She must have savored a cornucopia of memories, writing, "God . . . has let me see with my own eyes the good results of this desire."[8]

Indeed, she "had befriended Sioux Chief Red Cloud, . . . overcome the hostility and indifference of society and the Church to establish an amazing network of schools, churches and missions specifically for blacks and Native Americans, [and been] a zealous visionary who was almost a century before her time in demanding civil rights for all."[9] At her death, more than five hundred of her sisters taught in sixty-three schools throughout the country.

When the magi came to welcome Christ in Bethlehem, they set an important precedent. Not only the poor and un-educated sought the Christian mission, but also the wealthy and educated. Drexel's background gave her the skills and confidence to address social inequality among minorities. A hundred years before such concerns were on anyone's radar, she took the initiative, arousing public interest. Katharine was canonized in 2000, the second native-born saint after Elizabeth Seton.

Questions for Reflection or Discussion

What do you think motivates a wealthy socialite who'd traveled in her own private railroad car to shift to a life of poverty and simplicity? Do you see anyone today doing anything similar? If so, describe.

Further Readings

Peter Finney Jr., "The Legacy of St. Katharine Drexel," *St. Anthony Messenger* (October 2000), http://www.americancatholic.org /messenger/oct2000/feature1.asp.

Kathleen Jones, *Women Saints: Lives of Faith and Courage* (Maryknoll, NY: Orbis, 1999).

8

Rachel Carson

If I had influence with the good fairy who is supposed
to preside over the christening of all children I should
ask that her gift to each child in the world be a sense of
wonder so indestructible that it would last throughout
life, as an unfailing antidote against the boredom and
disenchantments of later years, the sterile preoccupation
with things that are artificial, the alienation from the
sources of our strength.

— Rachel Carson

Rachel Carson is perhaps the least overtly religious of
anyone in this book, yet her work was inspired by a
powerful reverence for God's creation. As one biographer
says, "her attitude towards the natural world was that of a
deeply religious person."[1] Her respectful life and writing
echo the psalmist's belief: "The earth is the LORD's and
all it holds, / the world and those who dwell in it. / For
he founded it on the seas, / established it over the rivers"
(Ps 24:1-2).

Born in Springdale, Pennsylvania, in 1907, Rachel loved exploring the outdoors. Her mother, who loved books and wildlife, encouraged her daughter, and became that key adult she describes in *The Sense of Wonder*: "If a child is to keep alive his inborn sense of wonder . . . he needs the companionship of at least one adult who can share it, rediscovering with him the joy, excitement and mystery of the world we live in."[2] When her mother died at age eighty-eight, Carson would pay tribute: "more than anyone else I know, she embodied Albert Schweitzer's 'reverence for life.'"[3]

Rachel had always wanted to be a writer, and prepared for that in college, until she was required to take biology in her sophomore year. She found it so intriguing, she majored in zoology. Her career would later combine her two passions. As her editor Paul Brooks explains, "The merging of these two powerful currents—the imagination and insight of a creative writer with a scientist's passion for fact—goes far to explain the blend of beauty and authority that was to make her works unique."[4]

Her summers, spent studying at the Woods Hole Marine Biological Laboratory, were her introduction to the sea, which would remain a lifelong fascination. Even before she saw it, she longed for it as a child. Again, the lines of psalms weave through her life: "The voice of the LORD is over the waters; / the God of glory thunders, / the LORD, over the mighty waters" (Ps 29:3). It would also become the subject of her first book, *Under the Sea Wind*, received, as she said, "with superb indifference" and disappointing sales.[5]

Carson's personal life, by her own admission, was often full of tumult. During the Depression, Carson's father's death was followed soon after by her married sister's. Carson and her mother then raised her nieces, Marjorie and Virginia, and when Marjorie died, Carson (almost fifty) adopted her son, Roger, then aged five.

This great-nephew figures prominently in her book *The Sense of Wonder*, where she describes wrapping him, as an infant, in a blanket and taking him to the beach in the "rainy darkness." "Out there, just at the edge of where-we-couldn't-see, big waves were thundering in, dimly seen white shapes that boomed and shouted and threw great handfuls of froth at us. Together we laughed for pure joy— he a baby meeting for the first time the wild tumult of Oceanus, I with the salt of half a lifetime of sea love in me. But I think we felt the same spine-tingling response to the vast, roaring ocean and the wild night around us."[6]

Carson was the sole support of this family, and she often dealt with financial problems. After completing her master's degree, she worked for the Fish and Wildlife Service in Washington, DC. One of the first two women hired as anything but secretaries, she eventually became its biologist and chief editor.

Her work provided hard scientific data underlying her delight in the natural world. She saw no conflict between her belief in evolution and her belief in the Creator: "Believing as I do in evolution, I merely believe that is the method by which God created, and is still creating, life on earth. And it is a method so marvelously conceived that to study it in detail is to increase—and certainly never to diminish—one's reverence and awe both for the Creator and the process."[7] Her attitude recalls Thomas Merton's, who when frustrated with pompous church services or contentious meetings would rejoice in the woods around his hermitage, praying "the psalms of the rain, of the odors and crackling of the fire, / the psalms of the stars and the clouds and the winds in the trees— / all equally eloquent."[8]

By 1952, Carson was able to resign from her job because of sales from *The Sea Around Us*. This immensely popular book, geared to the nontechnical reader, won the National Book Award, stayed on the *New York Times* best-seller list for eighty-six weeks, and was translated into twenty-eight languages around the world. Humanity depended on the sea, yet people knew almost nothing about the mysteries in its depths. Carson explored that world with zest, explaining, "If there is poetry in my book about the sea, it is not because I deliberately put it there, but because no one could truthfully write about the sea and leave out the poetry."[9]

Profits from the book enabled her to buy a cottage in Maine on the water's edge, where she'd spend the summers and write. She felt that to stand by the edge of the sea, watching the running of eels and shad, "is to have knowledge of things that are as nearly eternal as any earthly life can be."[10] She loved watching the ocean and birds, exploring the tidal pools, passions she'd share with Roger. Their experiences together of delight in the natural world provided the foundation for her writing that helped countless concerned adults introduce children to this source of unending beauty, power, and creativity. ("Help Your Child to Wonder" appeared initially as a magazine article and became a book after her death.)

She and Roger hated leaving, each fall, the Maine summer home where she could say with the psalmist, "Pleasant places were measured out for me; / fair to me indeed is my inheritance" (Ps 16:6). Rachel knew the connection between human spirituality and the human home on earth. "I believe natural beauty has a necessary place in the spiritual development of any individual or any society. I believe that whenever we destroy beauty, or whenever we substitute something manmade and artificial for a natural feature of the earth, we have retarded some part of man's spiritual growth."[11]

That sensitivity explains why Carson was so keenly alert to dangers no one else noticed. Many chemicals had been developed during World War II to halt insect-borne diseases. As early as 1945, she had misgivings about the indiscriminate use of insecticides. But DDT was effective in eradicating malaria globally, and by 1959, eighty million pounds were used in the United States. This and other highly toxic chemicals had been developed for war, with no testing of their effects on other life forms. Carson saw a direct parallel to radioactive fallout—both contaminated the entire ecosystem. The word "environmental" wasn't even used at the time, but Carson was one of the first to see the complex web of relationship between all living things and their habitation.

Carson's own reverence for life stood against an unquestioned reverence for industry. After all, the production of chemicals was a huge force in reviving the economy after the war. Naively, most Americans believed that some murky figure in the government would protect them from poisons in the atmosphere and water. Carson blew the whistle on these false assumptions: "The more I learned about the use of pesticides, the more appalled I became. I realized that here was the material for a book. What I discovered was that everything which meant most to me as a naturalist was being threatened, and that nothing I could do would be more important."[12] Knowing that she would cause a furor, Carson nevertheless spoke with the bravery and clarity of an Amos or Jeremiah. She believed it her duty, following Abraham Lincoln's words, "to sin by silence when they should protest makes cowards of men."[13]

Carson's authority was questioned because she had three strikes against her: she didn't have a PhD, she wasn't associated with an academic institution, and her degrees weren't considered prestigious in the scientific world. At a time when people were greatly concerned about external enemies that could destroy the country, she drew attention to the "enemies within."[14] She boldly challenged a key assumption of her era: "better living through chemistry." Ironically, she was diagnosed with breast cancer in 1960, wrote *Silent Spring* during debilitating surgery and radiation that left her exhausted, and died in 1964, aged fifty-six, eighteen months after its publication.

Treatment for cancer at that time was grueling and largely ineffective. Most patients would crawl into bed afterwards, depleted. Truly a pioneer, Carson would pause, recoup her strength, and then continue the audacious challenge, the daring adventure. She even saw the positive side of interruptions: being away from the text for a while gave her a better perspective on it. When her energy would return, she'd write with delight, "I do seem . . . to be riding the crest of a wave of enthusiasm and creativity."[15]

She was already an expert at research, and the fame of her previous work opened doors. In response to her requests, a "mountain" of information poured in from around the world; she put it together like a jigsaw puzzle. For instance, a professor at Michigan State University observed and documented the "spectacular decline" of birds on campus as a result of intensive spraying for Dutch elm disease. "Yet the disappearance of birds was but one obvious indicator of an underlying peril of greater dimensions; the slow poisoning of the entire environment, of which man himself is a part."[16] Many physicians contributed extensive research on hazards as poisons entered body cells. Dr. Hueper of the National Cancer Institute named DDT a "chemical carcinogen"— frighteningly present in breast milk.

Carson pointed out how self-defeating chemical spraying was: mosquitos simply developed a resistance, requiring more toxic chemicals to kill them. As she said in a letter to her publisher, "the mosquito has the last laugh, for while we have been progressively poisoning our own environment, the mosquito has been breeding a superior race composed of individuals that are immune to chemical attack."[17]

It took four years to complete the book, but Carson felt serene about the long gestation because her scientific facts were solid and her foundation unshakable. Because she was an artist, she could make the material accessible and compelling; because she was a scientist, she could make it unassailable. *Silent Spring* became "one of those rare books that change the course of history."[18]

Predictably, the book's publication brought an onslaught of criticism orchestrated by the chemical industry—a small but wealthy sector of society. As Terry Tempest Williams, an eloquent naturalist herself, says, "Spinster. Communist. A member of a nature cult. An amateur naturalist who should stick to poetry and not politics. These were just some of the labels used to discredit her. Rachel Carson had, in fact, lit a fire on America's chemical landscape."[19] Some critics attacked things she hadn't said; others hadn't read the book.

Fortunately, Carson also had a brief glimpse of success. Hearing that the *New Yorker* planned to serialize *Silent Spring*, she wrote her best friend Dorothy Freeman: "I said

I could never again listen happily to a thrush song if I had not done all I could [to preserve it]. And last night the thoughts of all the birds and other creatures and all the loveliness that is in nature came to me with such a surge of deep happiness that now I had done what I could—I had been able to complete it."[20]

And people responded enthusiastically, pleased they could understand a book that had translated scientific jargon. The book sold sixty-five thousand copies in its first few weeks, and became a Book-of-the-Month Club selection. During a press conference in 1962, President Kennedy announced that the Department of Agriculture and Public Health Service would examine the issue "particularly, of course, since Miss Carson's book."[21] Few can appreciate the importance of this investigation, because state and federal governments used pesticides extensively. For the first time, laypeople took ownership of their woods and streams, and held government accountable to protect them. Although environmental issues are complex, "one shudders to imagine nonetheless how much more impoverished our habitat would be had Rachel Carson not sounded the alarm."[22] Thanks to her, spring may be quieter, but the "dawn chorus" of birds is not completely silent.

Meanwhile, she realized the intense irony of her rising success as her health declined: "I keep thinking—if only I could have reached this point ten years ago! Now, when there is an opportunity to do so much, my body falters and I know there is little time left." Yet with great wisdom, she saw her own death through the lens of her studies on life cycles: "It is a natural and not unhappy thing that a life comes to its end."[23]

The awards poured in: from the National Wildlife Federation, the American Academy of Arts and Letters, the Izaak Walton League. There were more invitations to speaking engagements than Carson could possibly accept, as the realization gradually dawned: she was *right*. A letter of praise from Trappist Thomas Merton said Carson had effectively diagnosed the ills of contemporary civilization. She described this human arrogance toward creation during a debate on CBS News: "We still talk in terms of conquest. We still haven't become mature enough to think of ourselves as only a tiny part of a vast and incredible universe."[24] Although she never referred to the book of Job, her attitude was similar to God's wry amusement, asking the bewildered human, "Where were you when I founded the earth? / . . . who laid its cornerstone, / While the morning stars sang together / and all the sons [and daughters] of God shouted for joy?" (Job 38:4, 6-7).

Before her death, Carson contemplated her unique form of immortality, writing her friend E. B. White, "It is good to know that I shall live on even in the minds of many who do not know me and largely through association with things that are beautiful and lovely." In this as in so many things, she was prophetic. Terry Tempest Williams wrote in 2002 that because of Carson's influence, "I want to know the grace of wild things that sustains hope."[25]

Fittingly, she lives on in many ways. *Time* magazine named her one of the most influential people of the twentieth century. The Nature Conservancy, a beneficiary of Carson's will, has preserved parts of the Maine coast called the "Rachel Carson Seashore," and the Department of the Interior has named a wildlife refuge there in her honor. Less tangible is her effect on so many children who lived after her. A role model for painstaking research, international collaboration, women's role in science, and sheer, joyful wonder at God's design, it's appropriate that Carson have the last words here:

"Those who dwell, as scientists or laymen, among the beauties and mysteries of the earth are never alone or weary of life. Whatever the vexations or concerns of their personal lives, their thoughts can find paths that lead to inner contentment and to renewed excitement in living. Those who contemplate the beauty of the earth find reserves of strength that will endure as long as life lasts . . . There is something infinitely healing in the repeated refrains of nature—the assurance that dawn comes after night, and spring after the winter."[26]

Questions for Reflection or Discussion

If you were talking to a young woman interested in a career in science, what might you tell her about Rachel Carson?

What would you tell Carson about the state of the environment now?

Further Readings

Paul Brooks, *The House of Life: Rachel Carson at Work* (Boston: Houghton Mifflin, 1972).

Rachel Carson, *The Sense of Wonder* (New York: HarperCollins, 1998).

Esther de Waal, *A Seven Day Journey with Thomas Merton* (Ann Arbor, MI: Servant Publications, 1993).

Peter Matthiessen, ed., *Courage for the Earth: Writers, Scientists, and Activists Celebrate the Life and Writing of Rachel Carson* (Boston: Houghton Mifflin, 2007).

William Souder, *On a Farther Shore: The Life and Legacy of Rachel Carson* (New York: Crown, 2012).

9

Dorothy Day

Love and truth will meet;
  justice and peace will kiss.

— Psalm 85:11

B ill and his wife have worked with the poor for over
twenty years, training young volunteers to work in
some of Denver's most challenging homeless shelters, bat-
tered women's homes, child care facilities, and soup kitch-
ens. Asked whether Dorothy Day should be included in
a book on the US saints, he replies earnestly, "Of course
she didn't want to be a saint. But what matters more is, *we*
need her now."

He'd only begun to touch on the contradictions that
surround this woman. But based on that one sincere vote,
here's Dorothy. She believed, after all, that "there are many
saints, here, there and everywhere and not only the canonized saints that Rome draws to our attention." At the
same time, she spurned formal canonization for herself,
not wanting "to be dismissed so easily."[1]

It was almost as if Dorothy Day found the notion of sainthood had grown distant and irrelevant. Briskly, practically, as she did everything, she dusted it off and made it serviceable. In a world of violence, social upheaval, and war, she called for saints who would disarm the heart. To those who condemned "the enemy," she offered a quiet reminder that all humans were temples of the Holy Ghost and members, at least potentially, of the Mystical Body.[2]

She even redefined the notion of martyrdom—not gallantly standing before the firing squad, but the daily loneliness, shame, dying over the years. She'd seen it often in the "grey men" on the breadline: jobless, lifeless, resentful. To them she tried to restore housing, dignity, and hope.[3]

A casting director looking for saint material would've rejected Dorothy on multiple grounds: a leaning toward Communism, multiple relationships with men, an abortion, a child born out of wedlock, and frequent jail terms. Stir into the mix a narrow-minded church whose leaders wouldn't dream of listening to "radical" laywomen. The vast majority of Catholics at the time saw their role as following the rules, and were content to pay, pray, and obey. They were used to sermons, not homilies, asking for money, rarely touching on the Gospel. Day's call to see Christ in troubled faces shocked their rote conformity.[4]

With tongue happily in cheek, her 1936 letter gleefully summed up the gossipy accusations against her: "I'm supposed to be an immoral woman, with illegitimate children, a drunkard, a racketeer, running an expensive apartment on the side, with money in several banks, owning property, in the pay of Moscow, etc." As her granddaughter Kate Hennessy described the contradictions when meeting her grandmother, "To have known Dorothy means spending the rest of your life wondering what hit you." At the same time she gives you a home, she shakes the foundations.[5]

A final irony, given Dorothy's stance for peace: her canonization was proposed by Archbishop of New York John O'Connor, who had been chief of Navy Chaplains with the rank of admiral, and served the military for twenty-seven years.

Let's start with a brief summary of Dorothy's remarkable achievements. Early in her career, in her first visit to the South, she was shocked by the poverty in Arkansas. Never one to dither, she telegraphed Eleanor Roosevelt, the president's wife, also a lady who got things done. Mrs. Roosevelt contacted the governor, who—unsurprisingly—stonewalled.

But no amount of brisk bureaucratic subterfuge could stop Day for long. She plunged into writing because her father and brothers had been journalists. "After all," she said, "I had a typewriter and a kitchen table and plenty of paper and plenty to write about."[6] *The Catholic Worker* newspaper she edited and wrote skyrocketed from 2,500 to 35,000 copies printed in its first six months. By 1938 they'd reached 190,000 copies. Ever the writer, she first proposed houses of hospitality in print, but didn't actually begin one until a desperate young woman told her she'd been sleeping in subways with a friend, who in despair had thrown herself in front of a train.

Gradually, Dorothy and her helpers rented apartments and houses for the homeless. It was all rather ragged slum-living, with no staff receiving a salary. Yet in those first five years, more than thirty houses of hospitality were founded beyond the shaky, original New York beginning in Dorothy's apartment. "Today 227 Catholic Worker communities remain committed to nonviolence, voluntary poverty, prayer, and hospitality for the homeless."[7]

Her community's 1955 opposition to New York City's first civil defense drill might have initially seemed a silly reason for twenty-seven people to go to jail. But their view gradually became accepted: that it was impossible to survive nuclear war and ridiculous to practice hiding in subways or under desks. By 1961, over two thousand people gathered in "cheerful disobedience," the press editorialized about the futility of the drills, and the whole exercise became an embarrassment quickly abandoned.

So too Dorothy's first, unpopular instincts proved correct long-term in the civil rights movement, the Vietnam War opposition, and the farmworkers' unions. Willingly, she went to jail for her causes because she could see in prison a monastic cell, where stripped of everything, she could mystically share the lot of prisoners around the world.[8] Because she knew prison so intimately, she would gather people to sing Christmas carols outside the windows of the New York women's jail.

Despite apparent success in many arenas, Dorothy wouldn't be human if she didn't agonize over her deficiencies. For years after she and common-law husband Forster Batterham (her daughter Tamar's father) broke up, she hoped for reunion and marriage, and was honest about the pain of her "long loneliness." (Ironically, when Forster's partner of thirty years lay dying of cancer, who *else* would he ask to care for her than Dorothy?) In 1976, she complimented him on their thirteen great-grandchildren, "all . . . your progeny!"[9] Astonishingly, given his agnosticism, Forster led her funeral procession and appeared in the communion line there!

So many other demands called her away from motherhood, that she felt guilty for neglecting her daughter Tamar. In a 1940 letter she wrote, "I miss Tamar terribly—it's like a toothache."[10] She resisted her daughter's early (at age eighteen) marriage to David Hennessy, then watched the painful process as he became mentally ill and the marriage ended in permanent separation.

Constantly dealing with crisis at the Catholic Worker, Day wrote of her own impotence and irritation, the venom people directed toward her.[11] Even a few excerpts from her letters are enough to disabuse anyone of the idea that sainthood is a sunny stroll through a flowery meadow. She knew that when the Catholic Worker failed, it was often because of her explosive judgmentalism.[12] Like the rest of us who recognize bundles of contradictions within, she regretted events in her early life, and what seems a constant impatience with others. But she lived the Russian novelist Dostoevsky's line, "Love in reality is a harsh and dreadful thing compared to love in dreams."[13]

What made Dorothy tick? Surely a rich inner life that flourished despite the squalor in which she lived. "I am praying because I am happy, not because I am unhappy. I did not turn to God in unhappiness, in grief, in despair— to get consolation, to get something."[14] She turned to God with overflowing joy, just as her initial conversion came about because of her delight in Tamar. Her grandchildren provided much happiness as she aged—and they must've been proud she was bugged by the FBI!

Regular retreats were central to the Catholic Worker Movement. Since Dorothy knew the need to renew her own spiritual life, she made it a cornerstone of the work. She knew as well how little people were fed in parishes, and she criticized neglectful shepherds.

Knowing the church was corrupt, Dorothy wrote in 1969, "the Lord was seeking me out and I could not resist Him. And I found Him in the Church, in the Sacraments, life-giving and strength-giving, in spite of . . . the boring sermons, the incomprehensible and mumbled Latin, the Sunday Catholic, the wide gulf between clergy and laity, even the contempt for the laity which I often felt, and even heard expressed."[15]

In her final years, memory and hearing may have faded, but her prayer life remained vibrant. Much of it was quite traditional, despite the fact that in so many other areas she moved past established boundaries: Mass, preparation for Communion and thanksgiving afterward, reading the Office, saying the rosary, covering a long list of people she'd promised to pray for. Always, prayer seemed to be the deep well that fed the work of mercy.

Another life-giving source was beauty, especially to see it "from the dung hill of a slum."[16] One of Dorothy's favorite quotes was Dostoevsky's, "the world will be saved by beauty." She tried to live out Ruskin's "duty of delight." Throughout her life, she loved reading (Russian novels), opera (especially Wagner), films, and nature. Even in the squalor of the slums, she found and created beauty. Michael McGrath writes, "the creative acts of writing, composing, or painting are the best means we humans have of looking pain and suffering right in the eye and declaring ourselves free of their power over us." He also points out that when her staff were sick, she'd tuck them into bed with a good book and lovely music.[17]

Always delighting in her cottage on Staten Island where she'd lived with Forster, Dorothy wrote about the peace of the ride there on the ferry—"being upheld on the water reminded me of the 'everlasting arms' which sustain us."[18] The sea brought her calm and strength; wisely, she visited it often. Even a half-hour ferry ride (which docks in New York City near the first home of Elizabeth Ann Seton) brought the taste of salt spray, the wheeling arcs of gulls, sunset, silence, refreshment. Living with neediness, congestion, and often chaos, she turned to nature for quiet space.

Farms were central to the Catholic Worker mission. Because of her personal experience, Day valued the respite the land could offer overworked city staff. But many farms floundered when residents were more interested in talking than in working. Few had any rural experience, and they wasted time battling over trivia. Despite the closures, Dorothy could still write lyrically about an evening breeze in the apple trees. "There was a quiet and perfect peace and a happiness so deep and strong and thankful that even my words of prayer seemed inadequate to express my joy."[19]

Dorothy also encouraged religious art that wasn't soupy or sentimental. In contrast to the sanitized, drifting-above-the-earth Jesus and saints popular at the time, she invited Ade Bethune's and Fritz Eichenberg's illustrations for *The Catholic Worker*. In these, Christ stood in the breadline or in court before a judge, or worked hard at carpentry.

Reading between the biographical lines, Peter Maurin seemed an irritating, constantly talking prophet. Nonetheless, he was the visionary who gave Dorothy the practical steps she would enact: a newspaper, houses of hospitality, and farms. She survived Peter's early "indoctrination," sermons that began at 3:00 p.m. when she returned home from research at the library and continued until 10:00 p.m., when she insisted he leave. His vision of Catholic social teaching came just when she needed it. Her own faith was beginning to suffer from observing hypocrisy in church leadership, their contempt for or avoidance of the poor.

When *The Catholic Worker* needed money at the beginning, she made the ultimate sacrifice: pawning her typewriter. When the paper proved popular and people donated more than the penny asking price, she got the typewriter out of hock. Enormously successful, the paper presented a new, salty voice that people hadn't heard in Catholic literature until then.[20]

What probably landed her and the Catholic Worker Movement in the most trouble was her firm opposition to war: even World War II, which seemed to many a legitimate cause. She saw the works of mercy as polar opposites of works of war: why clothe the naked one day, then burn them alive the next? House the homeless, then incinerate the city?[21] This pacifist stance made Dorothy an outcast from the Catholic community, even rejected by some Catholic Workers. Sales of the paper plummeted. For some fifteen years, she lived under a cloud. Then the Vietnam War began, and Catholic Workers were among the first to protest. Her refusal to participate in war, and willingness to pay the cost by going to jail, was finally making sense.

Her nonconformity was outspoken, fiery as some of the early Christians. Seeing photos of the young Dorothy and Forster on the beach, they seem so attractive, probably set to walk down the aisle like thousands of other couples in the 1920s. Perhaps their unconventional relationship laid the groundwork for Dorothy's different views of other widely accepted customs. Refreshingly earthy about her own sexuality, she wrote to Forster, "Sex is not at all taboo with me except outside of marriage. I am as free and un-suppressed as I ever was about it. I think the human body a beautiful thing, and the joys that a healthy body have are perfectly legitimate joys." Ironically, despite his refusal to marry, their relationship drew out her innate spirituality: "Through a whole love, both physical and spiritual, I came to know God."[22]

In an era of active "red menace" hatred, she openly declared, "I can say with warmth that I loved the Communists. I worked with and learned much from them. They helped me to find God in His poor, in His abandoned ones, as I had not found Him in the Christian churches."[23]

She was probably the first devout Catholic to join the picket line at Cardinal Spellman's chancery. Their relationship continued to be tumultuous as he supported the Vietnam War, and she pointed out the irony of "sprinkling holy water on scrap metal to be used for obliteration bombing."[24]

She knew that the church was a harlot, but also our mother. She wrote, "As a convert, I never expected much of the bishops. In all history popes and bishops and father abbots seem to have been blind and power hungry and greedy. I never expected leadership from them. It is the saints who keep appearing all through history, who keep things going."[25] She found so much richness in Catholic mysticism and spirituality, she didn't waste time lamenting the shortcomings of a human institution. Never did she glorify community, but, in a eulogy for a difficult resident, described "the heart rending and soul searing experiences we have in living together."[26]

Dorothy's clear-eyed pragmatism speaks to the twenty-first century. When a priest encouraged her to write more about the "joys of poverty," Dorothy could think only of a neighbor, widowed with nine children. The five-year-old had TB, from too much winter cold and too little food. Dorothy couldn't call that anything but grim endurance.[27]

Tensions, discouragement, and disagreements were common among Catholic Worker staff members. Dorothy even defused one crisis when a small faction wanted a paid professional staff to better publicize social justice. Some disliked Day's reliance on the advice of clergy and insistence on obedience to the local bishop.[28] Yet, her delicate dance somehow kept her in the good graces of the hierarchy—most of the time. Perhaps it's a badge of honor that she was often suspect by both the FBI and church leaders!

She seemed to have constant reality checks, when Maurin's somewhat airy philosophy hit the hard ground of experience. Reluctantly, she had to admit that the farms, to which they were initially devoted, really didn't constitute a main part of their mission. Still, she conceded the good: "We might not have established a model community, but many a family got a vacation, many a sick person was nursed back to health, crowds of slum children had the run of the woods and fields . . . , and groups of students spent happy hours discussing the green revolution."[29]

Asked about the large proportion of "nut fringe" attracted to the Catholic Worker, she responded, "if people are slightly mad, how much more attractive it is that they should be mad for God."[30] Perhaps Dorothy's greatest achievement, besides her devotion to her daughter and grandchildren, was the sustained, hard work of seeing everyone as a cathedral, an often improbable vessel for Christ.

Questions for Reflection or Discussion

Do you agree with Dorothy Day that "there are many saints, here, there and everywhere and not only the canonized saints that Rome draws to our attention"? Why or why not? Support your argument with evidence drawn from your experience or reading.

Imagine that you've been asked to report to Day on issues that were vital to her, updating her on progress since her death. What issues do you identify, and what do you say?

Further Readings

Dorothy Day, "A Friend of the Family: Mr. O'Connell Is Dead," in *Great American Catholic Eulogies*, ed. Carol DeChant (Chicago: ACTA, 2011), 171–79.

Jim Forest, *All Is Grace: A Biography of Dorothy Day* (Maryknoll, NY: Orbis, 2011).

Michael O'Neill McGrath, *Saved by Beauty: A Spiritual Journey with Dorothy Day* (Franklin Park, IL: World Library, 2012).

10

Thea Bowman

Over my head I hear music in the air. There must be a God somewhere.

—African-American Spiritual

Given the racism, ignorance, and lack of dialogue between races in the United States before the civil rights movement, it would've been easy for a young black woman in a white world to become embittered, despair, retreat within herself, take comfort in her extensive knowledge of literature. Instead, Thea Bowman did a great service to the North American church, coaxing people into a richer place where blacks and whites began to learn each other's languages—and not only the spoken ones, but the poetry of music, ritual, and movement.

As the grandchild of freed slaves, Bowman would probably not want to be remembered that way first. Instead, she'd say (or more likely sing) how she and others began the slow transformation of a stodgy, all-white, self-righteous, got-all-the-answers Catholic Church into one that began to see and value the gifts of other ethnic groups. Unexpectedly and magnificently, she turned the light of Franciscan joy onto the shadowy corners of racism.

As biographers point out, her timing was impeccable. An only child of doting parents, she could've basked in their love and her small town (Canton, Mississippi) forever. Instead, at the age of fifteen, Thea (her religious name; originally she was Bertha) staged a hunger strike to persuade her parents to let her join the convent. She grew so thin, her parents finally allowed her to enter the community of the Franciscan Sisters of Perpetual Adoration in La Crosse, Wisconsin. These women religious had a profound effect on her childhood, educating her at Holy Child Jesus Mission School. (Because no one would sell land for a black Catholic parish, it began in old army barracks on swampland called "frog hollow.")

Her parents had enrolled her there when they realized how miserably the public schools failed African-American children in the 1940s. Her dad, a doctor, and her mom, a teacher, appalled by the overcrowding and underfunding in the public system, transferred her to Catholic school in sixth grade. Like most of her classmates, Thea wasn't Catholic, but her learning escalated dramatically in an atmosphere of cooperation and excellence. Standards were high, and Bertha rose to meet them. She would always look back on the chance she'd been given there, a transition from wasting time to seeing herself as a learner in a vital community. In fact, she wanted to become like those sisters who had come to teach. When her father warned, "they won't like you," her spirited reply was, "I'll make them love me."[1]

Her thousand-mile train trip north, her first time away from Mississippi, could occur only because the sisters intervened. In those days, black people could ride only in the baggage cars. The sisters' negotiation allowed Thea to ride with the white sister accompanying her, in the passenger car.

For a girl who grew up surrounded by black people, the transition to the customs, music, and religion of whites must have been a culture shock far worse than white postulants experienced. (Throughout the state of Wisconsin lived only about five black people.) In a German/Irish community, no one was used to singing spontaneously or bringing Jesus into ordinary conversation. "Prim" and "proper" were the guidelines in the 1950s, when religion was a private and often silent matter! Imagine Thea's consternation when she progressed to wearing a *white* veil, the symbol of purity. How much she suppressed her natural style became clear only when it emerged in her adulthood.

Prejudice among other sisters, though not as blatant as "white only" drinking fountains in the South, still existed due to ignorance and inexperience. Only to trusted classmates could Thea whisper jokes about their being pale and anemic. When others might have wavered, she was grounded in her parents' love. (To them, she wrote, "It's awful chilly up here and I'm not just talking about the weather.")[2] From a strong inner core, unscarred by racial lunacy, she could later proclaim, "I thank God for making me my black self." She was proud that her people had remained loving, despite centuries of oppression.

Initially, Bowman desperately wanted to conform, to become like the sisters who had traveled so far to touch her childhood. So the first black member of the community soon became their poster child, for her wit, intelligence, and charm. When she progressed to teaching, white parents at first protested. Then they discovered what a dynamo she was in the classroom. It quickly became a badge of honor to be one of her students.

After years of successful teaching, especially at the college level, and the completion of her doctorate in English at the Catholic University of America, Thea emerged as her own person. In Washington, DC, she'd seen an emerging black consciousness and awakened to her own intrinsic gifts. No longer would she deny strong feelings; she became fully expressive and empathetic. Breaking out of the habit, freeing herself from others' expectations, and donning traditional African clothes, she became unstoppable.

Like flowers that flourish in tundra or other unlikely conditions, she may have found the bigotry a spur, not a stoplight. Traveling through her hometown with other white sisters, Thea had to crouch down out of view to avoid violence. And this brilliant, gifted woman could register to vote only because she was accompanied by federal marshals. Never vengeful, Thea persisted in her signature song, "This Little Light of Mine." And how she shone . . .

To her great delight, Thea became a charter faculty member of the Institute for Black Catholic Studies at Xavier University, a major center for the black Catholic movement in the United States. From 1980 to 1988, she taught liturgy and preaching to those who'd minister in black communities. Students and other teachers there became her longtime colleagues and friends. Father J-Glenn Murray commented on her fearless outspokenness: "People either love her or loathe her. I decided it was altogether easier to love her. So I do."[3]

At a time of lynchings and murders during voter registration drives, she built friendships—with whites, Hispanics, Native Americans, and Asians. She saw herself as a bridge between races, because she believed it sacrilege to pray together without attempting bridge-building.

Through her work as director of Intercultural Awareness for the Diocese of Jackson, Mississippi, she presented African-Americans not as second-class or apologetic, but as forthrightly saying, "We're here with gifts to offer!" Most pungently she pointed out the vanilla boredom of most white worship: "I say the church needs folks like me, to 'liven it up' from being so dull . . . We're tired of this. It's okay for you, but don't impose it on *me*!"[4]

Again, the time was right. After the Second Vatican Council, the church became more open to innovation, more welcoming to difference. What had been a "white only" domain expecting uniformity suddenly became open to other ways of doing things. No longer did the "colonizers" have all the answers, but they began to appreciate the gifts of nonwhite cultures.

Key to Bowman's success were her soaring voice and graceful movement. Tall and attractive, she challenged her own people to be faithful to how good they were and to their Catholic faith. Despite the slave traders, the poverty and the discrimination, she praised their bonds with God and their ancestors. As her friend Sr. Addie Walker said, "She could reconnect you with your spirituality rather than have to try to replicate somebody else's. . . . In her presence your phoniness would have to fall away."[5]

Always at the heart of her talks (eventually over a hundred a year), music touched audiences at a level beyond the "head trip" and became her finest vehicle for intercultural awareness. Performance is key to black theology; her song was designed to bring out the songs of others.[6] Often she'd recruit and train local choirs to sing with her; a cursory look at their performances on YouTube is enough to register their delight. Later, when she was in enormous pain, only the singing could distract her. In every sense, she followed St. Francis the troubadour.

The National Catholic Youth Conference became one of many sites that invited her back annually. Audiences throughout the United States, Canada, the Caribbean, Hawaii, and Africa welcomed her with unbridled enthusiasm; jubilant standing ovations were the norm. For years, she maintained a travel/speaking schedule that would exhaust a woman in her twenties. When she appeared on *60 Minutes* with Mike Wallace, her national popularity skyrocketed. She would exult, "when all God's children come together, what a time!" And she didn't dance around the reality of prejudice: "We sit here and we're real nice today. But on a regular basis we can do a job on one another."[7]

Then came the breast cancer, which would eventually kill her, in the same year both parents died. She dealt with crushing blows by remembering how Jesus in pain "never said a mumbling word."[8] Treatment for cancer has advanced considerably since her diagnosis in 1984. Yet, she could joke about the radiation treatments giving her "certified radiant woman status."[9] When the disease progressed to her bones and became terribly painful, anyone else would've used the excuse to abandon an intense speaking schedule. With a few easily understood exceptions, Thea carried on, and her message became even more powerful, coming from a bald, weakened woman in a wheelchair. Her friend Fr. Clarence Rivers believed that keeping up the pace was due not to her energy, but to her artistry.

To her prayer, "let me live until I die,"[10] she seemed to add, "and let me have fun!" Then it wouldn't matter how long she had. There was a new urgency as she realized her time was limited, and couldn't be wasted on inconsequentials.

One of her most famous talks, to the US Conference of Catholic Bishops, turned old white men, often dour, into a rousing chorus singing, "We Shall Overcome," linked within each other's arms. Rarely if ever has such a meeting led to so many tears.

When she left Viterbo University in 1978 to care for her aging parents in Canton, Thea hated relinquishing her job as choir director. As the cancer worsened, she became unable to travel and lost her voice. But forty students from the choir traveled to the childhood home where she lived, squeezed into the living room, and sang her favorite spirituals. She rarely cried, but did at the singing of "Roll, Jordan, Roll" because it was so beautiful.

The director casually mentioned that they'd be stopping at McDonald's for lunch before they started the return journey home. As they ate, they noticed a car in the parking lot, Thea inside. Without a word, they surrounded the car and sang "Deep River" as a final good-bye.

After her death on March 30, 1990, at fifty-two, Thea became the first black woman ever honored by being on the cover of *America* magazine. In a memoriam published there, Mary Queen Donnelly wrote, "at a time of much division in the Church, Sister Thea possessed the charismatic gifts to heal, to bring joy."[11] She convinced a fractious, turbulent, multicultural bunch that if we knew each other's songs, we needn't fear each other.

Questions for Reflection or Discussion

If Thea Bowman returned today, how might she assess the state of racism in the United States?

Name *one* quality of Bowman's you find most attractive.

Further Readings

Michael O'Neill McGrath, *This Little Light: Lessons in Living from Sister Thea Bowman* (Maryknoll, NY: Orbis, 2008).

Charlene Smith and John Feister, *Thea's Song: The Life of Thea Bowman* (Maryknoll, NY: Orbis, 2009).

11

Adorers of the Blood
of Christ Martyrs

In the end, it is the reality of personal relationships that
saves everything.

— Thomas Merton

During springtime, a sense of abundance permeates the
Ruma, Illinois, center for the Adorers of the Blood
of Christ (ASC). Frogs plop bodaciously into the ponds;
a tortoise seems to have crawled out of the Amazon. The
air drifting over five hundred acres is scented with hon-
eysuckle. Magnolias and tulip trees bloom hugely. Tender cornstalks are several inches high, and it's not hard to
imagine butter melting over the grilled kernels at a July
4 barbeque. The labyrinth prayer walk isn't marked by
stones as in drier climates, but carved into the long grass.
Rain falls generously. Green wheat stretches across the
acres. Seeing the stalks could lead quickly to meditation
on the passage, "unless a grain of wheat fall to the ground
and dies, it remains just a grain of wheat; but if it dies, it

produces much fruit" (John 12:24). It may be crushed into flour, perhaps for Eucharist, or, over twenty years ago, to nourish five women with a most unusual story.

The contrast between peace and plenty here, and the unrest and scarcity from a bloody civil war in Liberia couldn't be more dramatic. From this quiet farm scene, missionary sisters stepped into a situation of bombs, food shortages, erratic electricity, grenades, rockets, rats, bucket baths from the rain barrels, eating boa constrictors, maniac military leader Charles Taylor, roadblocks, machine gunfire, armed rogue bands, corpses littering the roads, and child soldiers. One hint of their motivation comes from 2 Corinthians 9: "whoever sows bountifully will also reap bountifully . . . God is able to make every grace abundant for you, so that in all things, always having all you need, you may have an abundance for every good work" (vv. 6, 8).

A confidence grounded in such abundance must have brought the first missionaries to Liberia, a place that was not always so dangerous. The initial foundation in Grand Cess in 1971 provided a health clinic and women's sewing classes. For almost twenty years, despite privations, ASC sisters had many reasons to celebrate simple things; they knew how to throw parties and engage in thought-provoking conversation.

The civil war worsened in August 1990, food was scarce, and the sisters joined thousands of other refugees and missionaries in an arduous escape. Their convoy, joined by patients from the clinic, crossed the river to the

Ivory Coast in leaky canoes. What they'd call their "exile" extended until July 1991, when they returned.

As conditions deteriorated in Liberia, what drew the five missionaries *back* to the strife? Something touched them so deeply that their resolve to be a part of the solution in the midst of so much dissolution was strengthened. Out of the ordinary comes incredible courage.

Sister Barbara Ann Muttra, sixty-nine at her death, who had worked as a nurse in Viet Nam for the previous three years, would look back over her eleven years on the African west coast as a tropical idyll, where the people welcomed the sisters with dance, fruit, and celebration.

Her feud with the local mayor seems relatively mild in light of later violence. She wanted him to pen the cows and goats running loose, because their dung mixed with the mud where the children played, leading to sores and ulcers. He'd respond that the animals deserved respect and should wander freely. For two years they battled. Meanwhile, Barbara discouraged the common practice of driving off evil spirits by placing pepper in a newborn's mouth (which caused blisters) and mud on the umbilical cord, causing tetanus. Encouraging the parents' cooperation with baby clothes donated by friends in the United States, she eventually reduced infant mortality from 80 percent to 20 percent, from two deaths a week to two a year. After ten years, local people ran her clinic smoothly, so she began the process again in Klay.

Barbara's focus was always prenatal and infant care, perhaps because of her own vulnerability as a child. Her dad died when she was eighteen months old; her mother raised seven kids alone. After she moved to Gardnersville near the capital, Monrovia, Barbara would commandeer vehicles to bring Catholic Relief Services supplies (food, medicine, clothing) to the interior, where the war became most devastating. A vital link in the lifeline to hungry children, she'd bribe the guards at checkpoints with spearmint gum.

Sister Agnes Mueller, sixty-two, found the changes of Vatican II "unleashing" after twenty years smothered in a long habit and fourteen as a nurse. The first woman to graduate from the Aquinas Institute in St. Louis with an MA in theology, she wanted to teach Liberian women to read. As one responded, before Agnes came, "I didn't think I had a brain and could learn." Looking back over her years of service in Liberia, Agnes wrote, "I'm glad that I came. There have been learnings in pain, vulnerability and suffering, which I probably would not have allowed myself to experience in another place and culture."[1]

Sister Joel Kolmer, fifty-eight, had taught in the elementary schools of Iowa and Illinois for twenty-five years before her cousin Shirley encouraged her to try Liberia. Her bedrock characteristic was not to worry. A talented amateur artist, she also played guitar and danced. During a terrifying interrogation by a rebel soldier, she waved her red and white baseball cap embroidered "Slick Chick," her favorite nickname. Her friend Sr. Alan Wurth commented that Joel was fearless about returning: "It's impossible for fear and love to occupy the same place in one's heart."[2]

Sister Kathleen McGuire, fifty-four, had the serene, open face that might fit into her hometown, Ridgway, Illinois, "Popcorn Capital of the World." Under her direction as peace and justice coordinator, the Adorers of Ruma became the only Catholic organization in the area to defy the law and offer sanctuary in their houses to Cuban and Central American refugees in 1985. A PhD in education, Kathleen reflected on early lessons learned not from a retreat director, but from her mother. Feeling "holy" as an eighth grader on retreat, she'd neglected one of her chores, gathering eggs. Her mom briskly informed her that God wasn't interested in her prayer if she didn't do right at other times. In fact, walking around with the holy air of retreat was silly "when I couldn't even do the little work I was asked to do around the farm."

Drawing on that earthy beginning, she wrote in 1983, "For me, then, ministry can only be the sharing of the gift that was given to me. However and wherever I am, my work, like the Father's is to breathe a little life into those I know, help them to come to be a little more fully, a little more freely who they are. And knowing, then, their own grace and beauty, be able to guess at the beauty and graciousness of their Father."[3]

Despite studying Spanish in preparation for Latin America, Kathleen decided to join her friends in Liberia. Her stay there would last fourteen months, during which she was constantly bitten by fire ants. She tried to view it as a camping trip, but her work was deadly serious. Many students at St. Patrick's High School in Monrovia had been forced to kill in the civil war. Given glue to sniff to numb them to violence, some were even forced to rape family members to prove their manhood and loyalty. Kathleen worked with their PTSD, but there were "so many human needs. So easy to fulfill some; so nearly impossible to meet others."[4]

Sister Shirley Kolmer, sixty-one, loved Liberia because the gap between her front teeth was considered a sign of beauty there. A PhD in math, she taught it at St. Louis University, and first went on a Fulbright to the University of Liberia in 1977 and 1978. Then she served as provincial from 1978 to 1984. Her vision was of "loving the comfort, but ready to get up and go at a moment's notice—women who dream dreams and continue to promise."[5] During the time she served in leadership, the community welcomed and housed refugees at the provincial house, and opened the residence for elderly sisters in nearby Red Bud to their parents and relatives too. Tall and persuasive, she convinced a reluctant leadership to let her and her cousin Joel return first to Liberia, after their "exile," setting up a home for the others. Her decisive argument: Terrible conditions were exactly the reason they *should* return. The convent they'd left six months earlier was riddled with bullet holes, and looters had left little furniture.

She served as principal of St. Patrick's High School, *energized* by the job's demands. At St. Anthony's Parish in Gardnersville, she was the 1992–93 "Mother of the Year." "She didn't have to be a biological mother. She did everything as a mother for the children," explained an African neighbor.[6] Charles Taylor's rebels had recruited child soldiers as young as ten, and revived ancient practices of torture and mutilation. So Shirley started a counseling program for boys pressed into war, both perpetrators and victims. Unsurprisingly, when a gunman threatened them, Shirley was the spokesperson who pleaded unsuccessfully for their lives.

During an assault on Monrovia launched by Taylor's rebels in October 1992, Sisters Barbara and Joel agreed to give one of their security guards a ride to check on his family. Driving there, two soldiers "jammed" a ride with them, meaning they asked a favor that can't be refused. Soldiers from the other faction must have seen them, fired on the car, and killed everyone in it.

Meanwhile, the three sisters at the convent were flattening themselves on the floor to escape bullets fired through their windows. Then armed men of Taylor's force came to their gate, demanded they come out, and shot Sisters Kathleen, Shirley, and Agnes.

When the first three caskets were returned to Dover Air Force Base, two ASC sisters were there to meet them. They observed how reverently the military flight crew stood at attention—not a requirement, but a show of respect for the sisters. It was echoed in the condolences of a twelve-inch stack of mail arriving daily at Ruma for weeks afterwards. More than $60,000 donated by St. Louisans went toward the education of Liberian women.

Father Jim Gessler was "like family" with the sisters, who persuaded him to use an inclusive language lectionary in his Liberian parish. He thinks they'd "laugh and say, 'we happened to be at the right place but at the wrong time—the same as thousands of others killed around Monrovia.'"[7]

William Twaddell, US ambassador to Liberia, confirming the deaths in a telegram to the Ruma provincial on October 31, 1992, wrote that the sisters were "acting in the most noble tradition of their order and their faith. The safety and welfare of the wounded and the defenseless motivated them and were their only concerns in the midst of war."[8]

Father Mike Moran, SMA, who wore a bulletproof vest and helmet to reclaim the sisters' remains, adds, "They would want people not to dwell on their deaths too much, but let it be like a sacrifice for peace."[9]

Sister Kathleen Reid's eulogy compared each to a source of light—Barbara a durable flashlight, Joel a dazzling sparkler, Agnes the reader a reading lamp, Kathleen a camping lantern, and Shirley a powerful bonfire—bathing all with warmth.

In 2010, Sr. Raphael Ann, ASC, returned to Liberia for a two-year commitment, fulfilling the local prophecy: "You sisters can never leave us because your sisters' blood is in our ground. You can't take that back. So this will always be your home."[10] At the twentieth anniversary celebration in 2012, Sr. Barbara Jean Franklin said, their martyrdom "was an invitation to stretch and widen our hearts . . . We, too are making salvation history. It's not just the big stuff, but every person we meet and every choice we make . . . Imagine all the light being squeezed through the cracks of our broken hearts onto the waiting world."[11]

A memorial sculpture by Rudy Torrini, which stands in front of the Ruma center, shows five women facing outward in a circle, their hands linked. Their heads are lifted; their stance is buoyant. In concrete form, it shows Rilke's concept of circles that widen as they reach around the world. The sculptor describes his work: "I kept the design to the utmost simplicity because in Liberia that is how the sisters lived their vocation. The women stand in a circle which is symbolic of their unity as well as their crown of martyrdom. Theirs was the ultimate gift in a time which is all about getting."[12]

Asked, "What made them tick? Why would they *return* to Liberia after such a dangerous escape?" the sisters who knew them well respond, "If there were five martyrs, there were probably eight motives." The words "pious" or "prissy" never come up. "Bold" and "tenacious" are more likely to surface. They had practical work to do: teaching poor, illiterate women; staffing medical clinics; counseling; feeding the hungry. (By 1990, forty thousand civilians in Monrovia had died of starvation.) Over and over, one hears of a love for the Liberian people, the drive to meet their needs and share their lot. Perhaps explaining motives is as hard as putting into words the reason why one loves a spouse or a child.

Clearly, they moved beyond the comfort and content of Ruma to a larger world, part of a scrappy sisterhood that also serves in Guatemala, Korea, and Bolivia. Their focus is "to bring the reconciling presence of the Blood of Jesus" into health care, education, and social services. They try to "approach all persons with great respect so that they . . . discover their dignity because they are worth the Blood of Christ."[13] Their persistence also characterizes an ASC sister who, as principal of an East St. Louis school, got garbage collection where there had been none, and celebrated as merrily as the neighbors on the day the trash cans arrived.

In 2013, Sr. Anita Fearday, herself a missionary to Bolivia, at a ritual naming people who have been lights in the sisters' lives, called out loudly, "Shirley Kolmer, *Presente!*" Still, they endure.

Questions for Reflection or Discussion

Sometimes, the Catholic Church is accused of hypocrisy. How might the lives and deaths of the ASC sisters answer those charges?

Further Readings

Adorers of the Blood of Christ, "Love Poured Out for Life," http://www.adorers.org/whoweare/ourstory/Martyrs.aspx.

Marie Clare Boehmer, ASC, *Echoes In Our Hearts* (Red Bud, IL: Adorers of the Blood of Christ, 1994, 2012).

Charlotte Grimes, "Lives of Faith," *St. Louis Post Dispatch* (April 11, 1993).

Cesar and Helen Chavez, Dolores Huerta

People who have no hopes are easy to control.

—Michael Ende, *The Neverending Story*

The United States is a country filled with natural wonders, and many of the most spectacular are in California. Waves crashing along jagged coasts or frothing on golden sands, Yosemite's El Capitan towering over the Merced River, the late afternoon light brushing jade-green buds or scarlet autumn leaves on grapevines. Yet these sights savored by visitors are not part of many Californians' worldview.

Think instead of those laboring in the vineyards, without any biblical gilding: stooped over for long, hot days inhaling pesticides, postures contorted, spirits depressed, then returning to substandard housing with inadequate food and pay. Day after day that routine continues, with perhaps the slight variation of picking lettuce or strawberries. No hope in sight, the grimness seems unending; the human beings are almost invisible.

Until a young man named Cesar Chavez, who'd picked cotton as a boy in the San Joaquin Valley, helping his family of migrant workers throughout his childhood, emerges on the scene. Before the Great Depression, the family had owned their farm in Yuma, Arizona, and even their migration to tent-living in California hadn't tarnished their inherent dignity. When discrimination occurred, "we were the first ones to leave the fields if anybody shouted *Huelga* [strike] . . . it was the right thing to do."[1] That spirit laid the groundwork for his later career.

After two years in the Navy, Cesar returned home to Delano and married Helen, the mother of his eight children and the quiet heroine of this story. Their honeymoon was a tour of California missions, which they loved and revisited often, knowing they were sites of both "grace and disgrace."[2] Later the Franciscans there would give his movement much needed help; surely Fr. Serra would approve. Cesar worked in fields and lumberyards, apparently on the path to repeat the numbing routines of so many others. Until he met Fred Ross, a labor organizer who worked for Saul Alinsky's Community Service Organization (CSO), and Donald McDonnell, a priest who introduced him to Catholic social teaching.

It was as if a door cracked opened in "the way it's always been." Chavez volunteered to help Ross register voters, intrigued that poor people could move beyond assumptions that they were "slave labor" and utilize their power for change. He discovered how Gandhi had improved the lot of Indian peoples through nonviolence. Meanwhile, he devoured the books Fr. McDonnell offered, and couldn't get enough of their stimulating discussions. Their studies affirmed the hopes of migrant peoples: for trade unions, the right to strike, a just wage, and human dignity. Eventually, Cesar would move this vibrant theology off dusty library shelves and into the fields, shacks, jails, markets, and organizational meetings of farmworkers.

Furthermore, he combined the moral tradition with key aspects of Mexican-American religion: prayer, gospel values, solidarity, and devotion to Our Lady of Guadalupe. Her banner would fly over gatherings because "her presence transforms a march into a pilgrimage and a picket line for better pay and working conditions into an act affirming human dignity and human transcendence. . . . This is the power of popular religion: Ordinary events of life are linked to the sacred and are transformed."[3]

Mary wasn't the only woman central to the movement for justice. Chavez's mother and grandmother were what Fr. Virgilio Elizondo, an expert on the popular faith, calls "the best theologians of the . . . community."[4] Their teaching would permeate his thought, and women would always hold leadership positions, despite opposition from more "macho" members. "Without Dolores Huerta and the women of *la causa*, Cesar Chavez's dream of a union for farm workers would never have come to pass."[5]

Many regard Chavez as the more visible leader, and Huerta as the engine behind the scenes. They met because they were both involved with CSO, but he was so soft-spoken and unassuming, it took a while to get to know him. She compared him to a lamb among lions. She could roar loudly herself: bold and skillful at organizing, she worked for the CSO and, in 1960, was the only woman to testify before a California Senate committee hearing about the plight of farmworkers.

When Chavez announced he was leaving the CSO to form a farmworkers' union, Huerta quickly followed, writing, "We have a hell of a task in front of us, but I do not think the task is impossible."[6] She did not exaggerate: for the most part, workers were frightened, illiterate, mobile, and easily replaced. They were used to being treated as "beasts of burden," and knew the formidable power of the growers arrayed against them. For people who moved constantly, to band together or strike would require tremendous courage and sacrifice. They were the ultimate underdogs, for whom the nation would eventually rally. But no one knew that at the beginning. For Chavez and other leaders to challenge the "status quo" was an act of profound faith, startling boldness—and grace. The Spirit was moving among human beings.

Both Chavez and Huerta were unlikely leaders. He had an eighth-grade education, little experience of public speaking, and no money. He began the groundwork of organizing the farmers with his life savings, $1,200, a few small donations and loans, his wife Helen's tiny salary from working in the fields. Spouses of saints and heroes get notoriously short shrift, but Helen's contribution deserves high praise: during the early years, she woke at 4:00 a.m., worked a ten-hour day, earned 85 cents an hour, and cared for eight children.[7] When situations became complex and strikers turned violent, Cesar wrote, "It's very tough. I don't know if I can continue." But a few days later, "I spoke to Helen. I'm ready to go."[8]

He attracted growing empathy because, as one recruit said, he was "poor like us, dark like us."[9] And he was infuriated that the benefits provided workers by the National Labor Relations Act in 1935, allowing collective bargaining and strikes, didn't apply to field-workers. He expressed the irony: those who grew much of the nation's food couldn't afford to feed their own children.[10]

At the National Farm Workers Association's inaugural convention in 1962, Chavez was elected president and Huerta first vice president. Both leaders made tremendous personal sacrifices to launch the NFWA. Huerta was a single mom raising seven children on meager wages. When she had to send her children to school with holes in their shoes, she reminded herself that farmworkers did it all the time. She believed women made better negotiators because of their patience—and lack of ego trips.[11] One of her first victories was securing Aid to Families with Dependent Children (AFDC) and disability insurance for California farmworkers in 1963, "an unparalleled feat" for an era when young children routinely labored in the fields.[12]

The fledgling union was thrust into the spotlight long before they felt ready. Chavez wanted to do the long, slow

groundwork of speaking with workers personally and earning their trust before he asked them to bear the sacrifice of
a strike. However, when the Filipino grape workers struck
for fair hiring practices, better wages, and living conditions,
their leaders asked his union to join. Chavez was somewhat
reluctant, but couldn't resist the members' growing desire
for action. In 1965, they voted to enter the first of many
strikes, this one lasting five years.

Retaliation from the growers was violent, supported by
local sheriffs and police. But Chavez, like Gandhi and Martin Luther King Jr., insisted that strikers remain nonviolent.
When one sheriff forbade the use of the word *Huelga*, or
strike, Helen led a group who repeated it loudly—in front
of TV cameras. After their subsequent arrest was publi-
cized, people around the country protested the affront to
free speech and donations began to pour in. The boycott of
California grapes went national, and Walter Reuther, head
of the United Automobile Workers, joined, bringing the
support of his powerful union.

Meanwhile, Chavez wisely buoyed the spirits of the five
thousand strikers with frequent Masses, a Mexican cultural
center for theater, art, music, and dance, and a newslet-
ter that poked fun at the growers. He recruited volunteers
who'd been successful with nonviolent techniques in the
Southern civil rights movement. And in addition to the
strike and boycott strategies, he began the effective march.
Timed during Lent, it became a reflective pilgrimage from
Delano to Sacramento, the state capital about three hundred

miles away. As the march grew in numbers, Catholic and Episcopal bishops voiced their support; rabbis shared Passover with the marchers.[13]

The religious dimensions cannot be underestimated. As one minister who joined the march said, "I'm here because this is a movement by the poor people themselves to improve their position, and where the poor people are, Christ should be and is."[14] Altars fitted into pick-up trucks buoyed the peoples' conviction that claiming the rights due God's people was a just cause. One scholar explains these shrines that only farmworkers could've created: A hundred candles burn before pictures of Guadalupe, the Sacred Heart, other revered figures. Tinsel and Christmas balls add to the decoration. Roberto Garcia, leader of the vigil, laughed and told *National Catholic Reporter*, "it's a mixed-up Mexican shrine."[15]

Dreading the publicity of the march's arrival on Easter, and more decline in their profits, the Schenley Vineyards capitulated first, agreeing to a union contract. (It's heartening to imagine the smiles on tired, dusty faces all along the route. People who'd been invisible in the fields suddenly had prominence on the streets.) Though untrained as a lawyer, Huerta negotiated it, and later joked about her lack of background and her gender in a letter to Cesar: "Being a now (ahem) experienced lobbyist, I am able to speak on a man-to-man basis with other lobbyists."[16]

Huerta was also instrumental in merging two different unions, and with Chavez cofounding the United Farm

Workers of America (UFW). In 1968 and 1969, she worked in New York to organize the table grape boycott, later expanded to lettuce and Gallo wine. There, she also met Gloria Steinem, and learned more about the feminist movement.

Her arguments with Chavez could be fierce, but she considered them a necessary part of their collaboration. Beautiful and outspoken, she kept notes during one UFW board meeting and recorded fifty-eight sexist comments. "The boys" eventually became more careful of what they were saying, and reduced that number to zero.

She sounds like Dorothy Day when she regrets the amount of time her speaking, travel, and over twenty arrests for peaceful protests took away from her children. (She had her eleventh at age forty-six.) But as her daughter Lori remembered, mom said that our sacrifices "would help hundreds of other children in the future. Can you argue with something like that?"[17] Indeed, she spoke out especially strongly about the effects of pesticides on children in the fields.

During the sixties, the civil rights movement, despite King's best efforts, turned toward violence. Watts, Newark, and Detroit erupted in riots; King prepared for the '68 march on Washington. Fearing the demoralization and restlessness of his own people, Chavez began a hunger fast. He intended to redirect his cause toward nonviolence, sounding like Gandhi when he said, "If the strike means the blood of one grower or one grower's son, or one worker or one worker's son, then it isn't worth it."[18]

As the fast continued, it prompted enormous empathy: prayer vigils, others fasting in sympathy, donations, press coverage. King sent a telegram commending his bravery; Helen and Senator Robert Kennedy (a *compañero*) feared for Cesar's health and encouraged him to stop. Chavez continued fasting for twenty-one days, until he had lost thirty-five pounds and could barely stand. Kennedy joined the celebration at an outdoor Mass when Chavez first ate, and declared, "The world must know that the migrant farm worker, the Mexican-American, is coming into his own right."[19]

After the murders of King and Kennedy, who had both been so supportive of Chavez and his cause, he might have feared for his own safety, especially as he received many death threats. But he refused to arm his bodyguards, and from all accounts remained serene despite the climate of violence. Fearlessly, he'd walk through crowds spitting on him and calling him a "dirty little Mexican communist."[20]

He also protested the Vietnam War, in which a disproportionate number of Mexican-Americans were dying. Like King, Chavez called it a morally unjustifiable battle, "gutting the soul of our nation." His oldest son Fernando, with his father's support, went to court to achieve conscientious objector status.[21]

Finally, in 1970 after five years of boycott, more than twenty more growers signed an agreement with Chavez, who wore a white Filipino shirt in honor of those who had begun the strike. Growers agreed to increase wages, contribute to a health plan for workers, and place safety regulations on pesticides. As the workers sang victory songs, they were voicing a hard-won self-respect.

By 1971, Huerta had negotiated many important contracts, including restrictions on the use of DDT. She then helped enact California's Agricultural Labor Relations Act of 1975. Signed by Governor Jerry Brown, it finally allowed farmworkers collective bargaining for better wages and working conditions.

The next challenge was empowering lettuce and other vegetable pickers in the Salinas Valley, where Chavez went to jail for refusing to end a national lettuce boycott. That arena continued to be volatile because, with lettuce rotting in the fields, the growers would hire illegal Mexican immigrants. Chavez had great empathy for these desperately poor people, but also knew that their strikebreaking jeopardized the work of his union. By 1979, more than twenty-five thousand people marched on Salinas, where the culminating rally was attended by Brown, a supporter. There, a leading tomato grower agreed to raise pay to $5.29 an hour by 1982, which was a huge victory then. By tiny increments, the agribusiness system, which had seemed impenetrable, was changing.

The short-handled hoe, used for thinning and weeding, was outlawed by almost all growers outside of California. Readers may wonder why a hoe belongs in a book on sanctity. This tool caused workers to bend over all day, and led to such serious back injuries they nicknamed it "the devil's instrument." Chavez knew its effects firsthand; back pain from using it as a boy continued throughout his life. He put it graphically: "The short hoe is the nail they use to hang us from the cross."[22] Growers contended that without it, crops wouldn't be properly tended and they'd go bankrupt. In fact, as civil rights lawyers proved, the long-handled hoe was more efficient for plants and far less damaging to humans. When Brown's administration finally outlawed it, there were strong biblical echoes of Jesus healing the woman bent double (Luke 13:10-17).

During the eighties, some of the high spirits of the movement's early years began to erode. There was dissension in the ranks; many union staffers simply couldn't afford to work for the low wages Chavez paid. (He himself never earned more than $6,000 a year.) Meanwhile, a Republican governor was elected with the help of over a million dollars from agribusiness.

Chavez continued his fight against pesticides into the nineties, speaking at colleges and fighting in court, trying to convince people not to eat grapes until they were free of deadly chemicals. Yet even now, according to the Environmental Protection Agency, 300,000 of the nation's 2.5 million farmworkers are poisoned to some degree each year.[23]

Like anyone else in this book, Chavez had his flaws. Long work hours and dedication to the cause frequently kept him away from his family. Some critics believe he became paranoid later in life, refusing to delegate responsibility.[24] While Chavez had personified the high spirits and inspired the goals of the movement, he was less adept at the gritty chores. "What he had not done is prepare for the transformation of the movement into a working organization."[25] But one reason he undertook fasts was always to do penance for his own shortcomings.[26]

Like everyone else in this book, his heroism sprang not from worthiness or achievement, but from God's free gift. Asked what kept him going, he answered, "It's difficult to explain. I like to think it's the good Spirit asking me to do it."[27] At a time when many Hispanic people were locked into a hopeless dead end, he slowly opened a door to a brighter path, from exploitation to independence. They increased control over their own lives and enhanced their dignity. In pragmatic terms, the work of the union raised farmworkers' wages from less than $2 an hour in the mid-'60s to over $5 an hour thirty years later.[28]

In 1993, at age sixty-six, Chavez returned to his birthplace near Yuma, Arizona. He testified against the same agribusiness giant that had seized his family's land and caused their migration to California. He fasted to give impetus to his testimony in court; some believe that might have contributed to his death during his sleep. (In 1996, UFW won the case.) A year after his death, Chavez was awarded the Presidential Medal of Freedom posthumously; Helen received it for him from President Clinton.

In "Elegy for a Hero," Douglas Foster describes the funeral: "On the dais behind Cesar's coffin, an indigenous troupe is dancing during a break between prayers. We're moving down an aisle, surrounded by the cultural cacophony Chavez represented. Rhythmic clapping builds to a crescendo as cries of 'Si, se puede!' 'Viva Cesar Chavez!' and 'Viva la union!' alternate with prayers in Spanish and English and a hymn promising Chavez's rebirth. 'Resucitó resucitó,' a priest sings."[29]

Huerta worked for thirty years with Chavez, and then continued after he died. In 1996, she organized twenty thousand strawberry workers in the Salinas Valley. While she was protesting against the policies of George Bush in his presidential run, a San Francisco police officer beat her with a baton, breaking four ribs and shattering her spleen. Public protest led to a policy change regarding crowd control and police discipline; Dolores was awarded an out of court settlement. In 2012 President Obama gave her the Presidential Medal of Freedom. As of this writing, she continues to advocate, spunky at age eighty-four. She sums up a lifetime of fearless, exhausting work: "I think we showed the world that nonviolence can work to make social change."[30]

Even now, the UFW's work remains undone. "The conditions for farmworkers today are unfortunately very much as they've been throughout the decades," commented the current president Arturo Rodriquez.[31]

Were Cesar, Helen, and Dolores saints in the traditional sense? This side of eternity, no one knows for sure. But it can be said with certainty: They had the compassion of Christ; they carried complex tensions without lashing out; they inspired and sacrificed. They believed in God's fidelity to God's people, and enacted it. They invited all people to join their work for justice, even if it simply meant avoiding grapes. They invited even their adversaries, the growers, to change, since by dehumanizing their workers, they dehumanized themselves.[32] Insults and humiliations were heaped upon them, but they did not return these in kind. Instead, they walked an often barren road with joy and peace. Their names will be honored for generations after them. *¡Que Vivan!*

Questions for Reflection or Discussion

According to theologian Karl Rahner, "ultimately in this world there is no finished symphony."[33] How might that be true for the work of the Chavezes and Huerta? (To better answer this question, it might help to look at the UFW website, http://www.ufw.org, and compare what's happening now with what happened then.)

Further Readings

Roger Bruns, *Cesar Chavez: A Biography* (Westport, CT: Greenwood Press, 2005).

Frederick Dalton, *The Moral Vision of Cesar Chavez* (Maryknoll, NY: Orbis, 2003).

Nathan Heller, "Hunger Artist," *The New Yorker* (April 14, 2014): 73–78.

Dolores Huerta Foundation, http://doloreshuerta.org/dolores-huerta.

Richard Jensen and John Hammerback, eds., *The Words of Cesar Chavez* (College Station: Texas A & M University Press, 2002).

E. L. Thompson, *Cesar Chavez* (Chicago: World Book, 2007).

13

Mychal Judge

Mychal Judge's God says, "you're OK, kid." . . . In his company you would feel like breathing.

— Malachy McCourt

Picture a tall fire ladder, swaying slightly beneath the weight of a man poised at the top. He clings to it with one hand; with the other, he clutches the skirts of his brown Franciscan habit. He is trying to reason with a man in a window who points a gun to his wife's head, holding her hostage. She holds their baby. Whatever the priest says worked. The gun was dropped, the lives were saved, and the Franciscan didn't fall off the ladder.[1]

That scene from Michael Duffy's funeral elegy for Fr. Mychal Judge symbolizes several frontiers where the latter stood, his roots firmly planted in the ground of New York. Someday it may seem mild, but a priest who openly admitted being alcoholic and gay, and rollerbladed in his sixties, was pushing the narrowly defined boundaries of priesthood in the 1970s and '80s.

124

At one time, Judge drank so heavily he had blackouts. The drinking began in the seminary with little sips of altar wine. By 1976, "his alcoholism had become so serious that it became both crisis and opportunity." After joining Alcoholics Anonymous, Judge later attended as many of its meetings as he could. Some thought he was more familiar with the AA book than with the Bible.[2]

The way he internalized AA's message is clear in these lines from their book: "We will intuitively know how to handle situations which used to baffle us. We will suddenly realize that God is doing for us what we could not do for ourselves."[3] It sounds like Judge's comment when he had to break bad news or counsel grieving families: "That's not me, Mychal Judge. That's the grace of God."[4]

One specific example occurred in 1996, when Judge heard about the crash of TWA Flight 800 off Long Island in which all 230 people aboard were killed. For more than two weeks straight, Judge drove daily from Manhattan to the Ramada Inn near JFK Airport. There he spent twelve hours a day consoling friends and families who had lost loved ones. He also celebrated Mass every other day, participated in counseling sessions for people of all denominations, and organized ecumenical memorial prayer services for the victims' families and TWA personnel. He commented, "When that call came through it was the Lord calling me somehow."[5]

Fr. Austin McCormack, principal of a sabbatical program in England Judge attended, said, "Like St. Francis he found

so much good to celebrate because he expected to find it—
and he went looking for it."[6] While in England at the Franciscan International Study Center, Judge scheduled an AA
meeting there. The risk was dramatic at a time when "if a friar
had trouble with drink, it was hushed up or he was sent away
for therapy." But AA had given Judge a way to understand
his own wound and transform it to help others. His friend
Brendan Fay said, "Within the recovery movement, he
found a community of people, a safe space where he could
be himself for the first time in his life. Slowly and surely,
all the things he had hidden or denied about himself were
in the open and the real Mychal Judge could find a home
for himself."[7]

So too for his second frontier: being gay. Judge openly
supported and ministered to gay people even at a time
when Archbishop John O'Connor was quoted in the *New
York Post* as saying, "[I would] close all my orphanages
rather than employ one gay person."[8] "Deeply pained" by
the prejudice against gays, Judge inaugurated the St. Francis AIDS ministry on Thirty-First Street. This daring initiative occurred when the misunderstanding of contagion was
so rampant that few priests would get near victims—even
dentists wouldn't see them. Michael Meenan, also gay and
alcoholic, said meeting Judge "was a godsend because he
was living proof that I was not a freak of nature."[9]

With Franciscan practicality, Judge would massage
the feet of AIDS patients who acutely felt rejected by the
church, asking, "Is there so much love in the world that

we can afford to discriminate against any kind of love?"[10] At first hesitant to march in New York's first inclusive St. Patrick's Day parade in 2000, Judge received wild acclaim from the crowd—and nervous disapproval from the church.

That continued when he was reported to the diocese for not wearing vestments at firehouse Masses. Judge told the young clerical bureaucrat who called him on the carpet, "If I have ever hurt [the church I've served and loved so dearly for forty years], I would like to be burned at the stake on Fifth Avenue at the front doors of St. Patrick's [Cathedral]." "No matter how many robes the cardinal [O'Connor] put on or how much power he tried to exert, he still could not . . . quash Mychal Judge."[11]

Just as St. Francis challenged the church of his day, Judge refused conventional notions of holiness. His friend Richard Rohr commented that Judge would laugh at "some of the mistakes of the order and the church—and some of their pretentiousness. He did not get angry. He just smiled at it. That was very Franciscan."A man like Judge whose morning prayer was "Lord, keep me outta your way" couldn't waste time on pious prattle. Instead, he admitted honestly, "We don't have any sure answers. We grope. We grow."[12]

And we do it with humor. Friends celebrated Judge's appointment in 1992 as chaplain to the New York Fire Department with a special lunch. Tom Ferriter said in his invocation, "Here's to Mychal Judge's Brooklyn Irish mother, who got everything she wanted in life: a son with a Roman collar and a city job."[13] Admiring the Statue of Liberty, Judge often wondered how his parents had felt, emigrating from County Leitrim, Ireland, full of hope on their arrival at Ellis Island.

Known for his "Brooklyn pugnaciousness,"[14] Judge was convinced that New York was the most fantastic place to live. He relished the stroll across the Brooklyn Bridge, and ironically, watched the Twin Towers being built.

The bold, pioneer spirit he'd inherited from his immigrant parents permeated his entries into worlds once thought closed to priests. "What marked out his holiness was precisely his refusal to inhabit any niche of conventional sanctity."[15] For all those efforts, he surely deserves to be included in the company of US saints. So the way he died seems almost like gilding the lily.

The story is well known: Judge rushed to the World Trade Center to be with the firefighters responding to the 9/11 disaster. Some speculate that he removed his helmet to pray the last rites over a dying firefighter, was struck on the head by debris, and died. Five rescue workers carried him out through the rubble; Shannon Stapleton's photo of them was widely published. (His friends joked that even in death, Mychal still loved a photo op.) Firefighters laid Judge's body before the altar in a nearby church, covering it with a sheet, his stole, and his badge. His eulogist pointed out how appropriate it was that Judge died first; then he'd be in heaven to meet over four hundred first responders who arrived later.

Judge's biographer comments on the impromptu ritual of two cops praying over his body at Ground Zero. It's not only OK for laity to give last rites in an emergency. It "was, in fact, entirely in keeping with Father Mychal's own sacramental theology of hallowing the moment and was typical of the way ordinary people generated light in the darkness of that day."[16] The overflow crowd outside Judge's funeral proved what his eulogist said: "When he was talking with you, you were the only person on the face of the earth. . . . We come to bury his heart but not his love. Never his love."[17]

In another interview, Michael Duffy added, "Countless people told me that on birthdays, anniversaries, dates of sobriety—whatever—they would get a little note from him. He must have kept a *huge* calendar! In everyone's lives, whatever was significant, he'd write them a little note about it or give them a telephone call. Everyone considered him family." A homeless man in the funeral crowd commented, foreshadowing Pope Francis, "That priest didn't hide in the sanctuary; he brought the sanctuary out to us."[18]

Questions for Reflection or Discussion

If you were to meet Judge for coffee at a New York diner, what would you like to say to him? What might he respond to you?

How was his manner of dying thoroughly consistent with his way of living?

Further Readings

Michael Duffy, "The Happiest Man on Earth: Chaplain Mychal Judge, NYFD," in *Great American Catholic Eulogies,* ed. Carol DeChant (Chicago: ACTA, 2011), 35–43.

Michael Ford, *Father Mychal Judge: An Authentic American Hero* (New York: Paulist, 2002).

14

Dorothy Stang

We can't talk about the poor. We must be poor with the poor, and recapture a tender and kind relationship with Mother Earth. Then we will know how to act.

— Dorothy Stang

Dorothy Stang may win the prize for going to the furthest frontier, the remote jungles of Brazil. From a happy childhood and early religious life in Dayton, Ohio, it may seem like a long trajectory. But not if one understands Dorothy. A gutsy idealist, she had always wanted to be a missionary. Arriving there with her friend Joan Krimm in 1966 was a dream come true.

Since Brazilian law required that everyone living there had to be Catholic, Portuguese slave traders would baptize each slave on the ship.[1] Often that splash of water was about as deep as the faith penetrated. It's embarrassing that after 400 years of Catholicism in Brazil, they have 18 million homeless and the largest gap between rich and poor of any country in the world. By 1974, greedy loggers and ranchers had destroyed 40 million acres of invaluable rain forest, a process that continues. This extraordinary gift of God's creation contains 30 percent of the world's biodiversity. Worse, the wealthy landowners treat their workers like slaves, and exploit them heartlessly.

Seeing the children's malnutrition and the people's ignorance of their rights ignited Dorothy. She worked with women to establish base communities, and even delivered—in a jeep—a baby who was named by her mother "Maria Jeepa."[2] In Anapu, she built thirty-six schools in thirty-six years, and then insisted the teachers get the government salary required by law. Perhaps most importantly, she upheld the dignity of human beings constantly threatened by the police, military, or landowners.[3]

Although the government granted poor farmers parcels of land, the loggers and ranchers would inevitably burn their small homes and crops, so the wealthy could clear land for more lucrative grazing and beef production. With the land sharks bribing the police, anyone who protested could be killed without penalty. Meanwhile Stang spoke out loud and clear: "We can't talk about the poor. We must be poor with the poor."[4] And she was, often living with a family who had only enough room for her to hang her hammock above the dirt floor.

But Dorothy had studied Brazilian law, and had no problem calling federal officials to accountability. They would let her wait for hours, and then treat her condescendingly. Impatient with their stonewalling, she would sometimes dig into their files to find the protests they denied receiving. Any small victory loomed large, such as farmers blockading a bridge until the government finally fixed the road.

On her home visits, Dorothy would get medical treatment for worms, study life-giving subjects like creation spirituality, enjoy parties and ice cream. She came downstairs for her golden jubilee wearing her usual uniform, a T-shirt and shorts. Other sisters pleaded, "surely for this day, you could wear a skirt?" Her happiness seemed unassailable; she was doing what she loved in Brazil and was eager to return.

Only in later years do her letters reveal some ambiguity. Progress seemed slow; the poor were getting poorer and fighting among themselves.[5] She was growing tired, and her body older. After she turned seventy, long walks through the jungle became harder. Nonetheless, she continued arduous trips to Brasilia, reporting illegal logging. She was up against a hard fact: Brazil was becoming the largest cattle exporter in the world. With a booming logging business, the economy was improving. No government wants to impede that—and few officials wanted to hear the protests of "an old woman," as Dorothy termed herself. The $20,000 bounty offered by loggers and ranchers for anyone who'd kill her seemed astronomical to poor people.

At the same time she got death threats, with an irony that seems peculiar to Brazil, she received awards: the

Chico Mendes Medal and Humanitarian of the Year award in 2004. She continued to delight in unscarred rain forest, its green canopy her cathedral, and small reforestation efforts a joy.

One friend of Dorothy, Luis, encouraged other farmers to stay on land that was rightfully theirs. But the rancher Bida sent drunken henchmen to threaten Luis and his wife Francisca's seven children. Allowing the frightened family a little time to escape, the thugs then burned down his house and crops. Although Stang reported the crime to federal police, they had little interest in arresting anyone. Dorothy had a map that clearly showed the land belonged to Luis and other farmers, and planned a meeting with them for February 12, 2005.

She never got there. Beneath magnificent towering trees, two men confronted her on the path. She showed them her map, again explaining the farmers' rights. Asked if she had a weapon, she replied, "only one," and pulled out her Bible. She read aloud the Beatitudes, so her last words would have been "Blessed are the peacemakers, / for they will be called children of God" (Matt 5:9). What a graceful prelude to a violent death. Shooting her several times, the gunmen vanished.

Dorothy's body was left lying in the rain from about 7:30 a.m. until about 3:30 p.m. Local police investigated only reluctantly, but as the news spread internationally, the Brazilian president sent in two thousand troops to prevent more violence. Ordinary people grieved; ranchers and loggers exulted, thinking that after a few days the turmoil would subside and they could continue on their arrogant ways. They didn't anticipate the solidarity of crowds who were outraged, the banners demanding justice for the killing, the voices of human rights groups, lawyers, Notre Dame sisters and friends, the long series of trials.

Amid shouts of "Dorothy *Vive*!" she was buried in her favorite dress with a sunflower pattern. Saint Julie, the foundress of her order, had said, "Turn to God as sunflowers turn to sun." Certainly she had lived the Notre Dame motto, "Women with hearts as wide as the world."[6]

Questions for Reflection or Discussion

What parallels do you see between Kateri Tekakwitha, the Native American saint, Rachel Carson, and Dorothy Stang?

What might enable a person with a background like Stang's, raised with typical North American comforts, to be so happy with so little in Brazil?

Further Reading

Roseanne Murphy, *Martyr of the Amazon: The Life of Sister Dorothy Stang* (Maryknoll, NY: Orbis, 2007).

15

Varied Paths, "Glorious Nobodies," and Anonymous Saints

> It is a lesson we all need—to let alone the things that do not concern us. [God] has other ways for others to follow . . . ; all do not go by the same path. It is for each of us to learn the path by which [God] requires us to follow . . . , and to follow [God] in that path.
>
> —Katharine Drexel

Anyone seeking directions on a map website or application will discover many routes by different forms of transportation: bus, car, bike, foot, rapid transit. So, too, the saints have found multiple ways to God—or perhaps with vast creative power, God finds multiple ways to reach *them*.

Consider, for instance, the dazzling diversity between Junípero Serra, who poured energies into building a string of churches, and Thomas Merton, who wrote of the same building: "The church was stifling with solemn, feudal, and unbreathable fictions. . . . The spring outside seemed much more sacred. Easter afternoon I went to the lake and sat in silence looking at the green buds, the wind skimming the utterly silent surface of the water, a muskrat slowly paddling to the other side. . . . One could breathe. The alleluias came back by themselves."[1] Not that Serra didn't love the beauty of creation, but Merton's path here seems similar to Rachel Carson's.

North Americans continue to pioneer wildly diverse roads today: in the research hospitals that seek a cure for cancer, the labs that discover new ways to purify water or use solar power, the schools that encourage and educate neglected or traumatized children. They carve paths in subtler ways that are no less holy: the parents caring for the autistic child who try different ways each day to touch him, the artist or musician who gives audiences another way to see or hear, the mother trying a new recipe for the hungry kids, the spouse of the Alzheimer's patient, the scientists who discover alternate forms of energy and innovations to preserve the planet's resources.

The church's shorthand often refers to a puzzling group. For instance, St. Isaac Jogues "and companions." Did the unnamed ones not bleed as profusely, scream in as much pain, shake with as many convulsions when they were tortured? Or, in more peaceful terms, did the initial six and many sisters who later accompanied Marianne Cope not work as hard in the leper colony of Molokai? When her energies flagged, she probably still got up in the morning because they were all counting on each other. Father Palou, Serra's friend and biographer, shared the heartache and ordeals, but who's ever heard of him? Fifteen unknown sisters helped Katharine Drexel found her first school for Native Americans in 1894; by 1903, eleven Navajo women were nuns prepared to carry on her work.

And what about the Irish priests who defended Julia Greeley, or arranged for the early education of Augustine Tolton, who escaped slavery in Missouri as a child and became the first black priest? What of the Franciscans who, when Tolton was rejected by seminaries in the United States, sent him to Rome for education and ordination, or who supported Chavez's early efforts?

Americans love heroes, but sometimes we overlook the people who support the star. As Carol Flinders points out in *Enduring Grace*, we must "see the incandescent superstar for what it is, but . . . see the constellation in which it has come into being, too, the reverent and loving care that has surrounded and nourished it."[2] None of the figures highlighted in this book did it alone.

Theologian Elizabeth Johnson names the feast of All Saints the one for "'anonymous' whom the world counts as nobodies and whom the church, too, has lost track of but who are held in the embrace of God who loses not one."[3] The letters of Paul address all the early Christians as "saints," even when he gets frustrated with their angry feuding.

If the group convened around the table in the introduction were to meet again, they might discuss directions for the saints of today. In what arenas do we still need pioneers? Surely, in health care, immigration, poverty, the environment, rightful places for women in church and society, education, an end to human trafficking; the list is endless. And in many other fields, needs are still undefined. There the North American saints of tomorrow will shine. If we're alert, we might even notice them moving subtly among us now.

Notes

Introduction

    1. Thomas Merton, *New Seeds of Contemplation* (New York: New Directions, 2007), 128.

    2. Daniel Boorstin, *The Americans: The National Experience* (New York: Random House, 1965), 65.

    3. Ibid., 121

    4. Ibid., 213, 44.

    5. F. Scott Fitzgerald, *The Great Gatsby* (New York: Scribner, 2004), 180.

    6. Boorstin, *The Americans*, 223.

    7. Joan Chittister and Rowan Williams, *Uncommon Gratitude: Alleluia for All That Is* (Collegeville, MN: Liturgical Press, 2010), 68, 74.

    8. Letter to Gen. Vernon Prichard, August 27, 1942, quoted in Robert Edsel, *The Monuments Men: Allied Heroes, Nazi Thieves, and the Greatest Treasure Hunt in History* (New York: Center Street, 2009), 1.

    9. Marian Wright Edelman, "Marian Wright Edelman Reflects on Working Toward Peace," Architects of Peace Project, http://www.scu.edu/ethics/architects-of-peace/Edelman/essay.html.

10. Michael O'Neill McGrath, *Saved by Beauty: A Spiritual Journey with Dorothy Day* (Franklin Park, IL: World Library, 2012), xiv.

Chapter 1: Junípero Serra

1. Gregory Orfalea, *Journey to the Sun: Junípero Serra's Dream and the Founding of California* (New York: Scribner, 2014), 15.

2. Father Cuthbert, OSFC, *Life of St. Francis of Assisi* (London: Longmans, Green, 1914), 142.

3. Orfalea, *Journey to the Sun*, 63.

4. Ibid., 67.

5. Ibid., 114.

6. Ibid., 123.

7. Ibid., 165–66.

8. Ibid., 170.

9. Ibid., 178, 180.

10. Donna Genet, *Father Junípero Serra: Founder of California Missions* (Springfield, NJ: Enslow Publishers, 1996), 9.

11. Orfalea, *Journey to the Sun*, 236.

12. Ibid., 251.

13. Ibid., 249, 250.

14. Ibid., 235.

15. Ibid., 256–57, 259.

16. Ibid., 297, 298.

17. Antonine Tibesar, ed., *Writings of Junípero Serra*, vol. 4 (Washington, DC: Academy of American Franciscan History, 1966), 223.

Chapter 2: Elizabeth Ann Seton

1. Anne Flood, SC, *Grace & Courage: The Poetic Inner Stream of Elizabeth Seton's Writings* (Vail, CO: Diamond Tail Press, 2011), 25.

2. Joan Barthel, *American Saint: The Life of Elizabeth Seton* (New York: St. Martin's, 2014), 9.

3. Ibid., 106, 128.

4. Ibid., 91, 92.

5. Ibid., 102.

6. Flood, *Grace & Courage*, 75.

7. Barthel, *American Saint*, 109.

8. Flood, *Grace & Courage*, 80.

9. Barthel, *American Saint*, 121.

10. Robert Seton, ed., Letter to Julia Scott, in *Memoir, Letters and Journal of Elizabeth Seton: Convert to the Catholic Faith, and Sister of Charity*, vol. 2 (New York: P. O'Shea, 1869), 74.

11. Barthel, *American Saint*, 185.

12. Ibid., 206.

13. Flood, *Grace & Courage*, 89, 93.

14. Ibid., 91.

15. Ibid., 73.

Chapter 3: Pierre Toussaint

1. Francis Butler, "Saints without Cassocks: Reflections on Canonization," *National Catholic Reporter* (April 25, 2014): 12.

2. Arthur Jones, *Pierre Toussaint: A Biography* (New York: Doubleday, 2003), 47.

3. Ibid., 45.

4. Ibid., 143.

5. Ibid., 204.

6. Ibid., 128.

7. Ibid., 306.

8. Ibid., 310, 311.

9. Ibid., 308.

10. Ibid.

11. Butler, "Saints without Cassocks," 12.

Chapter 4: John Neumann

1. Br. John Neumann, "Bishop John Nepomucene Neumann: An American Saint," *Catholicism.org* (July 11, 2005), http://catholicism .org/john-nepomucene-neumann.html.

2. Ibid.

3. Ibid.

4. Ibid.

5. "St. John Neumann," *Catholic Online*, http://www.catholic .org/saints/saint.php?saint_id=70#wiki.

6. Ibid.

7. Ibid.

Chapter 5: Julia Greeley

1. Blaine Burkey, OFM Cap, *In Secret Service of the Sacred Heart: The Life and Virtues of Julia Greeley* (Denver: Julia Greeley Guild, 2012), 34.

2. Ibid., 28.

3. Ibid., 35.

4. Ibid., 49.

5. Ibid., 17, 12.

6. Ibid., 32, 29.

7. Ibid., 50, 55.

8. Ibid., 33, 70, 30.

9. Ronald Rolheiser, *Sacred Fire: A Vision for a Deeper Human and Christian Maturity* (New York: Image, 2014), 124–25.

Chapter 6: Marianne Cope

1. M. Davilyn Ah Chick, OSF, and Malia Dominica Wong, OP, *A Walk with Saint Marianne Cope of Moloka'i* (Syracuse, NY: Sisters of St. Francis of the Neumann Communities, 2013), 79.

2. St. Francis Healthcare System of Hawaii, "Saint Marianne Cope's Legacy in Hawaii," http://www.stfrancishawaii.org/mission/our-patron-saint/the-story-of-st-marianne.

3. Lisa Benoit, "Mother Marianne Cope: A Blessed Among Lepers," *St. Anthony Messenger* (July 2005), http://www.americancatholic.org/Messenger/Jul2005/Feature2.asp.

4. Chick and Wong, *A Walk with Saint Marianne Cope*, 76.

5. Robert Louis Stevenson, "Reverend Sister Marianne: Matron of the Bishop Home, Kalaupapa" (Kalawao, May 22, 1889), Sisters of St. Francis of the Neumann Communities, http://blessedmariannecope.org/quotes_note.html.

6. Chick and Wong, *A Walk with Saint Marianne Cope*, 37, 7.

7. Ibid., 13.

8. Ibid., 87.

9. Carol Ann Morrow, "Kateri Tekakwitha and Marianne Cope: Two New American Saints," *Catholic Update* (October 2012): 4.

10. Chick and Wong, *A Walk with Saint Marianne Cope of Moloka'i*, 91.

11. Ibid., 67.

12. Sisters of St. Francis of the Neumann Communities, Quotes of Blessed Marianne Cope, http://blessedmariannecope .org/quotes_note.html.

13. Benoit, "Mother Marianne Cope."

Chapter 7: Katharine Drexel

1. Kathleen Jones, *Women Saints: Lives of Faith and Courage* (Maryknoll, NY: Orbis, 1999), 269.

2. Peter Finney Jr., "The Legacy of St. Katharine Drexel," *St. Anthony Messenger* (October 2000), http://www.americancatholic .org/Messenger/Oct2000/feature1.asp.

3. Ibid.

4. Ibid.

5. Ibid.

6. Ibid.

7. Murray Bodo, OFM, ed., *Tales of an Endishodi: Father Berard Haile and the Navajos, 1900–1961* (Albuquerque: University of New Mexico Press, 1998), quoted in Pat McCloskey, OFM, "Mother Katharine Drexel and the Cincinnati Friars," *St. Anthony Messenger* (October 2000), http://www.americancatholic.org /Messenger/Oct2000/feature1.asp.

8. G. Scott Cady and Christopher L. Webber, *A Year with American Saints* (New York: Church Publishing, 2006), 522.

9. Finney, "The Legacy of St. Katharine Drexel."

Chapter 8: Rachel Carson

1. Paul Brooks, *The House of Life: Rachel Carson at Work* (Boston: Houghton Mifflin, 1972), 9.

2. Rachel Carson, *The Sense of Wonder* (New York: Harper-Collins, 1998), 55.

3. Brooks, *The House of Life*, 242.

4. Ibid., 18.

5. Mark Hamilton Lytle, *The Gentle Subversive: Rachel Carson, Silent Spring, and the Rise of the Environmental Movement* (New York: Oxford University Press, 2007), 55.

6. Carson, *The Sense of Wonder*, 15.

7. Peter Matthiessen, ed., *Courage for the Earth: Writers, Scientists, and Activists Celebrate the Life and Writing of Rachel Carson* (Boston: Houghton Mifflin, 2007), 6.

8. Thomas Merton, quoted in Esther de Waal, *A Seven Day Journey with Thomas Merton* (Ann Arbor, MI: Servant Publications, 1993), 82.

9. Matthiessen, *Courage for the Earth*, 135.

10. Ibid., 4.

11. Ibid., 145.

12. Ibid., 11.

13. William Souder, *On a Farther Shore: The Life and Legacy of Rachel Carson* (New York: Crown, 2012), 19.

14. Matthiessen, *Courage for the Earth*, 10.

15. Brooks, *The House of Life*, 261.

16. Ibid., 252–54.

17. Ibid., 268.

18. Ibid., 227.

19. Matthiessen, *Courage for the Earth*, 138.

20. Ibid., 13.

21. Souder, *On a Farther Shore*, 4.

22. Matthiessen, *Courage for the Earth*, 17.

23. Brooks, *The House of Life*, 314, 327.

24. Ibid., 318, 319.

25. Matthiessen, *Courage for the Earth*, 144, 145.

26. Carson, *The Sense of Wonder*, 100–101.

Chapter 9: Dorothy Day

1. Jim Forest, *All Is Grace: A Biography of Dorothy Day* (Maryknoll, NY: Orbis, 2011), 118, 304.

2. Ibid., 156.

3. Ibid., 216, 130.

4. Ibid., 173.

5. Ibid., 164, 337.

6. Michael O'Neill McGrath, *Saved by Beauty: A Spiritual Journey with Dorothy Day* (Franklin Park, IL: World Library, 2012), 44.

7. The Catholic Worker Movement, http://www.catholicworker.org.

8. Forest, *All Is Grace*, 205.

9. Ibid., 221, 288.

10. Ibid., 168.

11. Ibid., 171.

12. Ibid., 242.

13. Ibid., 219.

14. Ibid., 77.

15. Ibid., 312.

16. McGrath, *Saved by Beauty*, 47.

17. Ibid., 5, 77.

18. Forest, *All Is Grace*, 151.

19. Ibid., 148.

20. Ibid., 143.

21. Ibid., 158.

22. Ibid., 103, 73.

23. Ibid., 189.

24. Ibid., 195.

25. McGrath, *Saved by Beauty*, 61.

26. Dorothy Day, "A Friend of the Family," in *Great American Catholic Eulogies*, ed. Carol DeChant (Chicago: ACTA, 2011), 178.

27. Forest, *All Is Grace*, 119.

28. Ibid., 141.

29. Ibid., 149.

30. Ibid., 241.

Chapter 10: Thea Bowman

1. Charlene Smith and John Feister, *Thea's Song: The Life of Thea Bowman* (Maryknoll, NY: Orbis, 2009), 38.

2. Michael O'Neill McGrath, *This Little Light: Lessons in Living from Sister Thea Bowman* (Maryknoll, NY: Orbis, 2008), 32.

3. Smith and Feister, *Thea's Song*, 168.

4. Ibid., 181.

5. Ibid., 191.

6. Ibid., 287.

7. Ibid., 253, 254.

8. McGrath, *This Little Light*, 58.

9. Smith and Feister, *Thea's Song*, 195.

10. McGrath, *This Little Light*, 17.

11. Ibid., 283.

Chapter 11: Adorers of the Blood of Christ Martyrs

1. Charlotte Grimes, "Agnes: 'Glad I Came,'" *St. Louis Post-Dispatch* (April 11, 1993).

2. Marie Clare Boehmer, ASC, *Echoes In Our Hearts* (Red Bud, IL: Adorers of the Blood of Christ, 1994, 2012), 180.

3. Ibid., 132.

4. Grimes, "Kathleen: 'The Country Is at Crisis Point,'" *St. Louis Post-Dispatch* (April 11, 1993).

5. Boehmer, *Echoes In Our Hearts*, 57.

6. Grimes, "Shirley: 'Everyone Has Seen Too Much,'" *St. Louis Post-Dispatch* (April 11, 1993).

7. Grimes, "Lives of Faith," *St. Louis Post-Dispatch* (April 11, 1993).

8. Carol Zimmermann, "Leaders express shock over sisters' deaths," *Catholic Courier* (November 5, 1992): 4.

9. Grimes, "Lives of Faith."

10. Boehmer, *Echoes In Our Hearts*, 307–8.

11. Ibid., 311–13.

12. Ibid., 310.

13. Adorers of the Blood of Christ, http://www.adorers.org.

Chapter 12: Cesar and Helen Chavez, Dolores Huerta

1. E. L. Thompson, *Cesar Chavez* (Chicago: World Book, 2007), 38.

2. Frederick Dalton, *The Moral Vision of Cesar Chavez* (Maryknoll, NY: Orbis, 2003), 157.

3. Ibid., 36.

4. Ibid., 33.

5. Ibid., 71.

6. Thompson, *Cesar Chavez*, 98.

7. Ibid., 55.

8. Roger Bruns, *Cesar Chavez: A Biography* (Westport, CT: Greenwood Press, 2005), 60.

9. Quoted in ibid., 32.

10. Ibid., 36.

11. Thompson, *Cesar Chavez*, 96.

12. Dolores Huerta Foundation, "The Feminist Seed Is Planted," http://doloreshuerta.org/dolores-huerta/.

13. Bruns, *Cesar Chavez*, 52.

14. Ibid., 51.

15. Dalton, *The Moral Vision of Cesar Chavez*, 42.

16. Dolores Huerta Foundation, "The Feminist Seed Is Planted."

17. Thompson, *Cesar Chavez*, 104.

18. Bruns, *Cesar Chavez*, 60.

19. Ibid., 63.

20. Ibid., 79.

21. Ibid., 76.

22. Ibid., 92.

23. Ibid., 118.

24. Nathan Heller, "Hunger Artist," *The New Yorker* (April 14, 2014): 76.

25. Bruns, *Cesar Chavez*, 99.

26. Heller, "Hunger Artist," 78.

27. Dalton, *The Moral Vision of Cesar Chavez*, 162.

28. Bruns, *Cesar Chavez*, 106.

29. Douglas Foster, "Elegy for a Hero," The Fight in the Fields: Cesar Chavez and the Farmworkers' Struggle, http://www.pbs.org /itvs/fightfields/cesarchavez2.html.

30. Thompson, *Cesar Chavez*, 106.

31. Heller, "Hunger Artist," 78.

32. Dalton, *The Moral Vision of Cesar Chavez*, 169.

33. Karl Rahner, *Servants of the Lord* (New York: Herder and Herder, 1968), 152.

Chapter 13: Mychal Judge

1. Michael Duffy, "The Happiest Man on Earth," in *Great American Catholic Eulogies*, ed. Carol DeChant (Chicago: ACTA, 2011), 39.

2. Ford, *Father Mychal Judge*, 21, 28.

3. Bill W., "The Promises," *Alcoholics Anonymous: "The Big Book"* (Mineola, NY: Dover, 2011), quoted in ibid., 85.

4. Ibid., 158.

5. Church and Friary of Saint Francis of Assisi, "Fr. Mychal Judge, O.F.M., 1933-2001," http://www.stfrancisnyc.org/fr-mychal -judge-o-f-m-1933-2001/.

6. Ford, *Father Mychal Judge*, 96.

7. Ibid., 102, 75.

8. Ibid., 84.

9. Ibid., 180.

10. Ibid., 124.

11. Ibid., 148, 149.

12. Ibid., 30, 18, 64.

13. Ibid., 143.

14. Ibid., 79.

15. Ibid., 200.

16. Ibid., 11.

17. Duffy, "The Happiest Man on Earth," 38, 43.

18. John Bookser Feister and John Zawadzinski, "No Greater Love: Chaplain Mychal Judge, O.F.M.," *St. Anthony Messenger* (December 2001), http://www.americancatholic.org/messenger /dec2001/feature2.asp.

Chapter 14: Dorothy Stang

1. Roseanne Murphy, *Martyr of the Amazon: The Life of Sister Dorothy Stang* (Maryknoll, NY: Orbis, 2007), 25.

2. Ibid., 40.

3. Ibid., 46.

4. Sisters of Notre Dame de Namur, "Dorothy Stang Novena: Fifth Beatitude," http://www.sndohio.org/sister-dorothy/Dorothy -Stang-Novena.cfm.

5. Murphy, *Martyr of the Amazon*, 113.

6. Some information for this chapter is from David Stang, in discussion with the author, January 19, 2008, Denver.

Chapter 15: Varied Paths, "Glorious Nobodies," and Anonymous Saints

1. Thomas Merton, *Conjectures of a Guilty Bystander* (Garden City, NY: Doubleday, 1966), 269–70.

2. Carol Flinders, *Enduring Grace: Living Portraits of Seven Women Mystics* (San Francisco: Harper, 1993), 219.

3. Elizabeth Johnson, *Friends of God and Prophets: A Feminist Theological Reading of the Communion of Saints* (New York: Continuum, 1998), 250.